OUT OF ME

WENT

43 DEMONS

Antoinette Cannaday

Out of Me Went 43 Demons,
by Antoinette Cannaday
ISBN # 0-89228-111-1

Copyright ©, 1994
by Antoinette Cannaday

Published By **Impact Christian Books, Inc.**
for Antoinette Cannaday

Cover Art: SPB Studios

Printed in the United States of America

All Scripture verses have been taken from the
Authorized King James Scofield Reference Bible.

ABOUT THIS BOOK

From the Author

This book is true. It is my personal testimony intended to give a powerful and potent form of understanding about a subject you may never have considered. I have compiled teachings, personal experiences, and the unanswered questions, which psychiatry is usually expected to answer. Psychiatrists have admitted that their field is not an exact science. This book is exact!

This less-than-exact science has many unanswered questions about multiple personalities, abnormal behavior patterns, thoughts, voices and desires. I know because I am one who was diagnosed as having a so-called chemical imbalance in the brain, which caused mental depression and drove me to suicide. I have tried psychiatry, and I have tried deliverance. Psychiatry, the medical study, diagnosis, treatment, and prevention of mental illness, failed to heal me. Deliverance, the casting out of evil spirits, worked! I have had forty-three demons, with desires and personalities of their own, cast from my body.

Due to medical study of mental illness, psychiatrists are now able to conduct extensive testing to predict the outcome of a child's life. The results of these tests can determine whether he/she will be motivated to crime and what kind of crime is likely.

Ministers of deliverance have discovered that evil spirits, living in human bodies, influence people's thoughts, habits and conversations, and seek to control the person in which they live. Even babies have been born with evil spirits. These spirits influence children and babies at the most vulnerable points in their lives and continue their influences into adulthood. This demonic control has determined the outcome of many lives.

Why haven't medical studies found a cure for the mentally ill? Psychiatrists have admitted they have only limited answers, yet patients' lives continue to be controlled by pills and injections. Are the potent forms of medicine being given to mental patients the answer? Are they safe to consume? If so, why are so many being disfigured with twitching, contortion of the facial features, and speech impediment? Are these the kinds of answers we are seeking? Why are some mental patients well for a time, only to manifest the same problems all over again? What happens during the remission periods?

Law enforcement has concentrated its efforts on illegal drugs such as cocaine, crack, heroin, and marijuana. What about the legal drugs? Thousands are legally addicted to Valium, Tranzene, Librium, Percodan, Darvon, and codeine. If the medication is taken with alcohol, the risk of death is enhanced. This book contains alternative methods and solutions.

The answer to suicide is in this book. I will take you right to the moment of my attempted suicide, but I will not leave you there. You will visit the psychiatrist's office with me and discover psychology's solutions. After all the earthly answers are revealed, you will come with me into the deliverance sessions, into the church sanctuaries, and read what the demons had to say. You will also read how God's ministers responded to the demons' words and what they did to give me God's answers to my problems.

Have you ever asked why so much misery is in the world? Have you blamed God for it? Who is the real motivator of perverse sexual acts, such as homosexuality, incest, child molestation and rape? Are you a rape victim who has never been free of the unclean feeling those wounds caused? Does vivid imagination cause you to relive the nightmare over and over again?

The law has done everything it can to make you safe, yet fear has enclosed you! What can you do? Maybe your problem is different. Perhaps you are not the victim, but the offender? You desire to stop, but can't. Perhaps you actually enjoy what you are doing, or you know someone who does. Whether you are any of these people or none of them, this book is for you.

Compare for yourself the difference between psychiatry and deliverance. Know and understand how a man of God, standing on the authority of Jesus Christ, is able to cleanse a body of mental depression, suicide, and multiple personalities. Know and understand how psychiatry, which is founded on misconceptions and a less-than-exact science, covers up and compounds the problems of the mentally ill through medication.

"And ye shall know the truth, and the truth shall set you free," John 8:32. Because I have been set free, I desire to see the same for all God's creation. Through my writing, I am going to take you into the world of child molestation, adultery, mental depression, suicide, anger, hatred; the list goes on. Not only will you understand the hurt, the shame and degradation, you will also understand the freedom and joy of being set free. You will understand why many people continue to return to their sins.

Whether you are sinner or saint, this book is no respecter of persons. If you are a church member, missionary, teacher, pastor, or Holy-Spirit-filled, I strongly urge you to read this material. No longer are these problems limited to the world; they are occurring in the church today. Many mighty men and women called by God have been brought down by the methods of Satan.

I Timothy 4:1 states, "Now the spirit speaketh expressly, that in the latter times some shall depart from the faith, giving heed to seducing spirits, and doctrines of devils." These are the last days and God's word is being fulfilled.

If you are seeking knowledge or just browsing for reading material, this is it! You have made the correct choice. You may accept this testimony or reject it, but I assure you, you will never forget it. Weigh the evidence before you make your judgment.

Antoinette Cannaday

NOTE: All names in Part I of this book, excluding the author's, have been changed.

DEDICATION

Looking unto **JESUS CHRIST**, the **AUTHOR** and

FINISHER of our faith; this book is dedicated to

Bishop Roy Bryant, Sr., D.D.,

and to his loving wife,

Mother Sissieretta Bryant.

Without their labor of love and many hours of prayer,
this book would not have been possible.

IN APPRECIATION

THE BIBLE CHURCH OF CHRIST, INC.

Thank you for all the prayers and support

Many sincere thanks to

Mary Parker,

For her faithfulness in transporting me to
and from my deliverance sessions

and to

Montrose Bushrod

for reading my manuscript

MANY LOVING

AND

THOUGHTFUL MEMORIES

My parents

who believed the word of God:

*"TRAIN UP A CHILD IN THE WAY HE SHOULD GO,
AND WHEN HE IS OLD HE WILL NOT DEPART
FROM IT,"*

Proverbs 22:6.

CONTENTS

PART I

SEDUCTION OF MY SOUL

PART II

FREE AT LAST

PART I

SEDUCTION OF MY SOUL

I

HATRED FOR MEN

I hate you! I hate you! I hate all men! You're just using me and I hate you! Thoughts of hatred rang over and over in my mind. I lost all ability to speak or even cry out. The battle against hysteria was within, and there it remained. My hands balled into fists ready to fight. My twelve year old body tensed into an immovable position. *This can't be the way it's supposed to be. I have no knowledge of sex, but I am being exposed to it in the most horrible way possible: in a dingy rooming house with a man who is old enough to be my father.* Until a few moments ago he was my friend.

Why is he doing this to me? He said he loved me. If this is love I want no part of it. I hate love! I'll never let anyone love me again.! My mind did not cease to function even though my voice never uttered a sound. Hysteria almost surfaced only to be replaced by silent pleading and begging for help.

Where is my daddy? Come help me, Daddy! Please come get this man away from me. What was the use? Daddy didn't know where I was. Just hold on, Antoinette, it'll be over soon. You're a big girl now. Whatever you do, just don't cry. Nobody must know. Especially not Mommy or Daddy. You must not tell anyone, Antoinette. Keep it all inside. It's too dirty to talk about. It must be, because Mommy or Daddy never mentioned anything like this.

The closest Daddy ever came to telling us girls about the facts of life was telling us to be apples in the top of the tree. "Keep a very high standard," Daddy said, "then the young men will always look up to you." He added, "if we are apples at the bottom of the tree, then we will be prey to anything that comes along. Eventually we will get rotten and fall to the ground. Everyone will kick us around. No one wants rotten apples."

I never wanted to be a bad apple, Daddy. Now I am, through no fault of mine. No one will ever want me again because I've been used. I'm rotten and I'm dirty. At least at the top of the tree, nobody could reach me. Now anybody can. It's so unfair.

What had happened to my beautiful morning of shopping? All I wanted was a new hat and a pair of shoes for Easter. This morning began with so much promise. I awoke with the feeling of excitement any normal twelve year old would have during the Easter holidays. The thought of a new dress, shoes, and maybe even an Easter bonnet, was enough to make me lose control of my emotions. Excited as I was, I still had to be quiet. It was early; too early to get out of bed. I didn't want to wake up my four sisters. We all shared the same bed. I knew if I turned the wrong way or made the slightest wrong move, somebody was bound to wake up angry.

It was peaceful this time of morning. No yelling or arguing. Having ten brothers and sisters didn't give us the quietest house on the block. In this household, one had to take advantage of the quiet whenever possible. Needless to say, there wasn't much privacy either.

Not hearing the sound of Mom in the kitchen, I continued to let my mind wander. I knew Daddy was up and already off to work. He worked as a packer for a moving company, which meant very early hours. Moving people from place to place provided much overtime also.

Even so, sometimes, Daddy's paycheck didn't stretch quite far enough. We had to be supplemented by welfare from time to time. Yet, we always had enough to eat. We didn't have much else, but we had food, clothes, and as Daddy said, "a roof over our heads."

Today was going to be different! I was going shopping, alone! This was the first time I didn't have to tag along with all my brothers and sisters. Eleven children and two parents crowding a shoe store caused people to stare. Some were envious, others just curious. It was embarrassing at times, at least for me. I was a private person. Today I was going to enjoy my privacy. I was going to buy whatever I wanted, and I didn't have to worry about the money. This was my secret from my sisters and brothers. Won't they be jealous when they find out that our family friend came to take me shopping alone?

He had his own car and his own money. His name was Mr. Lee, and he liked me. Mr. Lee said I was a special child. He thought I looked grown up. I didn't think so; I figured I had a long way to go. But Mr. Lee was a grownup, and grownups always knew the answers. Besides, I liked him because he reminded me of my daddy. They looked like brothers, except Mr. Lee was taller.

"Nettie!" Mommy shortened my name. "It's time to get up!"

There goes my privacy. Why did Mom always have to call me first? There are more people in this house than me. Well, that's all right. Nothing is going to spoil my excitement. This is one morning I don't mind getting up early. I made a quick dash to the bathroom to get my bath.

Daddy always said, "Just because we're poor does not mean we have to be dirty. We can always be clean, because soap and water don't cost children anything."

That was good, because I sure used a lot of it. I liked to be clean. Daddy said, "Cleanliness is next to godliness."

If anybody knew that, it had to be my daddy, because he was a preacher. If Daddy said it, it was true; that was just the way it was. Mommy thought I was just like Daddy. I didn't mind that one bit. No sirree!

I was so excited I could hardly sit still through breakfast. After eating everyone did chores. Then we had permission to go outside and play. Except me, of course. I had an important engagement.

Mr. Lee picked me up right on time. I trustfully put my hand in his and went to his car. We had a long ride ahead of us to the garment district on East 116th Street. I felt so bubbly inside, I sang most of the way downtown. I could even picture my new dress and shoes. Mentally, I had myself dressed up real pretty. It was like a dash of cold water when Mr. Lee stopped the car along side the road of a deserted street. He asked me how I felt as he moved closer to me. I felt no fear because he wa an adult. Mommy and Daddy had taught us to respect our elders. Besides, he was my friend. I had nothing to fear. Mr. Lee said he had to tell me abut the birds and the bees. I listened, but I wasn't particularly interested in this kind of information. Even Mommy and Daddy didn't talk that way. He said he had to teach me about tongue kissing, just in case boys at school tried to make a pass at me. Then I'd be aware of what was happening and I'd know to push them away.

"After all," said Mr. Lee, "you should know how to protect yourself."

Ugh! I hated it! Who wanted somebody's tongue in his mouth? Mr. Lee would never have to worry about anyone tongue kissing me, because I didn't like it. After I promised not to tell Mommy and Daddy what I'd learned (because they wouldn't understand), we were on the way to our destination. East 116th Street, New York, here we come!

I never saw so many stores in one place! It seemed as if clothes were hanging all over the sidewalks. This was the most exciting time of my twelve years. I tried on one hat after another. Finally, Mr. Lee helped me make my selection. I didn't like it too much, but Mr. Lee insisted that it made me look grown up. I remembered my manners and shyly thanked him. The rest I kept hidden inside.

Then the shoes. I'll never forget the shoes. Black, shiny patent leather--so shiny I could see my reflection. They cost eleven whole dollars! I'd never had shoes for more than $2.99 in my entire twelve years. I could picture myself walking proud. I could barely wait for everyone in the church to see me. And Mommy will love them. I was so happy, I thought I would burst inside. I again told Mr. Lee thank you. I really wanted to jump up and down, but that would not have been lady-like. Mommy and Daddy taught us to always to act like well-mannered ladies.

It was getting late, so Mr. Lee bought me a hot dog and we headed for home, so I thought. Again, I was mentally dressed with my new Easter purchases, when suddenly Mr. Lee was parking the car in front of a huge brownstone building. He said this was where he lived. With a child-like curiosity and trust, I went upstairs with my friend. He directed me to the edge of the bed. He said he had to change his clothes. I wondered why because he looked fine to me. I never remembered seeing an adult in underclothes before, therefore, I was uncomfortable. I hung my head and stared down at the floor. Seemed like this should have been done in private or not at all.

The next few moments were a nightmare I tried to erase from my memory forever. It was a invasion of my privacy, and it produced an uncleanliness that no amount of soap could erase. Feeling dirty and used went to the very core of my being; it penetrated through the very depths of my mind. Immediately, hurtful and abnormal thoughts entered in. 'I'm dirty and I'll never be clean again' rang over and over in my mind and it left its impression in my heart.

Less than eight hours ago, I left home to go shopping for a new dress and shoes. Instead, my life became clothed with the worst uncleanness I could imagine. No amount of cleansing could help me now; I thought I would never be clean again!

II

I'LL NEVER BE CLEAN AGAIN

The ride home was the most miserable ride I ever spent in my life. Just this morning, the thought of riding in this car was so exciting. What a difference a few hours could make. My life would never be the same.

I glanced up just as Mr. Lee was parking the car in front of my home. I quickly opened the door and jumped out. I didn't need this man holding the door open for me under any circumstances. I took a deep breath before I took off running into the house.

"Hi, Mom, I'm home. Mr. Lee bought me a lot of soda and I gotta run to the bathroom." All in a rush the words came tumbling out of my mouth as I made a quick dash past Mommy into the bathroom. I quickly closed the door and leaned against it. The combination of the lie I'd just told, and running past Mommy at breakneck speed caused me to lose my breath. I hated lying like that. I didn't have to go to the bathroom. Daddy had told me a liar wouldn't tarry in the sight of God. I hoped God would forgive me, because I had to lie. I needed time to get myself together.

I wondered if Mommy would be able to tell that I had changed. Would she be able to see that I was dirty? I looked into the mirror. I still looked the same. The long braids were still hanging on both sides of my head with the fat braid on the top. My face was still scrubbed clean. My teeth were still white. My hands were clean. Even my dress wasn't wrinkled. How could I look so clean on the outside and feel so dirty inside? Maybe if I washed up I'd get rid of this unclean feeling. I ran the water slowly into the sink so Mommy wouldn't be aware of what I was doing. She'd wonder why I was washing instead of trying on my new clothes. Mommy knew anytime we children went shopping, the first thing we did when home was to dive right into our packages. If she even thought I was doing otherwise, she'd be suspicious. I washed so much I thought I would scrub my skin off. I remembered Daddy's words. "Cleanliness is next to godliness." Maybe if I repeated those words along with the scrubbing, it would help to get me clean.

The more I scrubbed, the more the thoughts kept coming. *I'm unclean, I'm unclean. I'll never get clean. I've been used.* My head felt as if it would burst from so many unkind and hateful thoughts. My mind raced, drastically looking for an answer to solve my problem. Maybe if I just called Mommy, she could get me clean. If anyone could, she could. She was a specialist at cleaning. I was on the verge of calling her when I realized I couldn't tell her. Nobody must ever know. I couldn't tell anyone. This was one problem I had to deal with myself. Never in my life did I feel so lost and alone.

What is wrong with this soap? It's the same soap I used this morning. It has to get me clean. It says so, but it's not working. This soap is a liar. Just like Mr. Lee. That voice in my head kept telling me I'm dirty. Gullibly, I accepted the thoughts in my mind, when suddenly I heard Mommy calling me.

"Nettie, are you going to stay in the bathroom all day? Come thank Mr. Lee for these things, and try them on so we can see how they fit."

How I hated Mr. Lee! *I hate all men!*

"I'm coming," I said as I opened the door and slowly stepped into the living room. There he sat in Daddy's chair with his legs crossed, smiling at me. He looked like the well-satisfied cat that had just swallowed the helpless canary.

I picked up the hat and tried it on. Earlier I thought I'd look so pretty in a new Easter bonnet. Now it didn't matter. It would take a lot more than a hat to make me pretty now. Mommy, very innocently, asked if I liked it. Quietly I told her yes. I tried on one shoe while Mommy appraised the shiny patent leather on the other one. She thought they were good shoes. Mr. Lee said they cost eleven dollars.

They cost more than eleven dollars. Because of those shoes I'm nasty and dirty. Mr. Lee didn't pay for them; I did. I paid a very high price. There isn't enough leather in the whole world to pay for what that man did to me.

I looked around to see if anybody heard me. My thoughts were screaming in my head. The hysteria I'd just felt came from within. Outwardly I was calm, while a battle raged within me. For the second time today I was fighting a losing battle within.

Why can't I say these things out loud? Can't somebody see I need to talk? I want to cry, but I can't cry and I can't talk. If I did, Mommy would know, and it would probably kill her. Daddy would probably kill Mr. Lee. My sisters and brothers would blame me. Everybody would hate me. It would be best if I just held my peace, forever. I would just have to get tough and hard. At least that way it won't hurt so much.

Mr. Lee glanced at the clock. He thought it was time to go home. I wondered how he could be so cool and content. All this torment in my mind, and he calmly states, "It's time for me to go home."

Where do I go? What do I do? I can't tell anyone. I can't share this with my sisters. I've been separated from them. I'm now different than they are. Mr. Lee didn't use them. He used me. Why did he do this to me? He caused my entire world to fall apart. I'm suffering so badly on the inside, and nobody even notices it. Why can't they understand? I wasn't like that this morning; I didn't have these nasty thoughts. I'm unclean.

After Mr. Lee left, I went into the bedroom to take a nap. I thought sleep would make me feel better. I awoke to the sound of my daddy's voice. I wanted to go in and speak to him, but just as I started into the living room, I hesitated. Maybe Daddy would be able to tell that I was dirty. He seemed to know everything. I decided I'd sneak past him and into the bathroom first, but he saw me.

"Is that you, daughter? Come here."

"Yes, it's me, Daddy. I was going into the bathroom." Instead I went into the living room. Daddy was proud of me. He told me I was a smart little girl, and he expected me to amount to something. My grades in school were excellent. I loved reading, writing and arithmetic. I didn't even mind going to church. I enjoyed working with my peers. As a leader among the young people, I could write plays, speeches, poems, and sometimes, even songs. Daddy said my gift would make room for me. I had dreams of writing a play that would be a huge success. Now everything was ruined.

"Bend down, daughter, and take off my shoes. This old man is tired." As I was unlatching Daddy's shoes, I reinforced my determination to never tell Daddy. Somehow I would work overtime in church and school to make him proud of me. He need never be ashamed of his little girl. I would be the brightest and the best apple hanging high in the top of the tree.

"Go ahead now, Antoinette, get washed for supper. Set the table for your mother, and tell everyone to come and eat." I went into the bathroom to wash. For the first time I couldn't. Something was restraining me. I no longer cared about washing my body. Again I thought, *I'm not clean. I'm dirty. It's not going to help. so why bother?* I looked at the soap and the washcloths. After running the water in the sink, I wet the cloth and soap, wrung out the cloth, and let the water out. I never washed my face or hands. The same thing happened the next night. I skipped my nightly bath. I didn't brush my teeth. Instead, I went straight to bed. No longer did "Cleanliness is next to godliness" mean anything to me. I wasn't clean, so I wasn't next to God. My twelve-year-old mind did a lot of thinking for the next few hours.

Huddled under the covers, I wondered if Daddy knew I wasn't at the top of the apple tree any longer. I was now just above the ground. 'Somebody go to me, Daddy. I was growing all nice and round and pretty. I was waiting to get ripe, waiting to be of full age, waiting for the right one to come along, and the right time. Instead, too soon a man came along and snatched me out of my haven. How do you explain that, Daddy? He used me and left me near the bottom of the tree. I am on a branch close to the ground where anything and anybody can have me. I'm scared down here, Daddy. I'm prey to anything that comes along' These thoughts circled round and round until I drifted to sleep.

The next morning, no one minded getting up early. It was Easter Sunday! Even under the circumstances, I was excited about this day. My play was being performed in our church this evening. We worked hard during rehearsals, and I made sure everyone memorized their parts.

At the breakfast table, Daddy said the extra-long grace, the one reserved for Sunday mornings. Just as I began to eat, Daddy said, "Antoinette, you half washed your face. You still have sleep in your eyes. Go wash your face over."

As I got up to wash, I wondered what Daddy could say if he knew I didn't half wash my face; I just didn't bother to wash it at all. This time I forced myself to wash. I didn't want to chance making him angry, especially not today.

We arrived at church early, a few minutes before ten. As Sunday School Superintendent, Daddy took care of the business of that department. He was also our teacher. For someone who couldn't read or write very well, he excelled as a teacher. We were well taught about the Bible. I later learned that Daddy was taught by the Spirit of God and not man. Whatever we needed to know for a perfect walk in life, Daddy could find in God's word. Some people said he was a fire and brimstone preacher. I didn't know what that meant. But I did know Daddy meant business.

Six p.m. couldn't come fast enough. I could hardly wait to direct our play. The big moment arrived and our entire program was a success. Daddy sat in the congregation with tears in his eyes.

That told me all I needed to know. He was proud of his children. I was happier than I had been in a long time. Yet, happiness has a way of changing with the circumstances. My circumstances got the best of me. In less than a week I was again in Mr. Lee's brownstone apartment.

On our way downtown, Mr. Lee asked me if I had told my parents anything. I didn't answer him right away. He needed to sweat about that one. Remembering Daddy's teachings about obeying our elders, I quietly told him I had not. My answer put him more at ease. With a little more confidence, he told me to move closer to him and give him a kiss.

Inside I screamed, *I don't want to kiss you. You're just a dirty old man. I won't do it. I don't even kiss my daddy. I hate you!* He was edging me closer to him. Parking the car on another side street, he kissed me while I thought I would choke. On the outside I was calm and obedient.

Soon after we arrived in the garment district, Mr. Lee offered to buy my underwear. That made me angry. No man was going to buy my underwear. That was my mother's job.

Aloud, I said, "No, thank you. I don't need any."

Satisfied with buying a new dress instead and a patent leather pocketbook to match the shoes, we headed for home. I was hoping we would go directly to my house. Danger was lurking in Mr. Lee's room. I could feel it. All my mental pleading did no good. A few moments later, we pulled in front of the huge brownstone building. As we walked past the desk, I couldn't help wonder if these people in the lobby knew what was going on. Did they think I was his granddaughter? Maybe they thought I was his daughter; he was the same age as my father. It didn't matter what they thought. I needed help. All these people nearby and no one knew I was in trouble. Not one person could hear my silent plea for help.

Calmly I preceded Mr. Lee into his room. This seemed my fate in life. If I had to endure it, I would. But I did not have to like what was happening, and nobody could make me love this man.

I started for the chair in the corner, but he directed me to the bed. He removed my dress so that it wouldn't be wrinkled. I felt numb within and without, and my only hope was that this ordeal would be over as quickly as possible. I learned to daydream my way through the unbearable situations. Little did I know that this time would be more degrading than the first.

Mr. Lee told me he was going to show how a man really proves his love to a woman. This was by oral sex. Never in my life have I felt so ashamed.

I tried to focus my mind on other things to get through the degrading experience. My mind went blank; not even daydreaming helped this time. My whole body went rigid as a board. My hands again balled into fists, ready to fight.

My eyes searched for something other than my situation.
I noticed the sunlight streaming through the window. Over
in the corner lay my dress on the back of the chair. My
shoes were resting in the same corner. Seeing them only
made me angry. Anger went through me as a heat wave.
I didn't care if I sinned or not. Even if I killed this man, so
what? He deserved to die. But I couldn't do that. I was a
little girl in a woman's position. I had only one
consolation:
anger.

The ride home was a silent one; a war was going on
inside my mind. Daddy's words came back to me. "If we
just didn't have to think, we'd be all right." I understood
now what Daddy meant.

Sometimes thoughts hurt. They hurt my mind and my
heart, and I couldn't even express them. *Please, somebody
help me. Somebody notice that something is wrong, and
tell my mommy and daddy.* I couldn't open the car door.
I might not survive. My mind said I'd be better off dead.
But I didn't want to die. I wanted to be free. The thoughts
reminded me the only way to be free was to die. I was not
going to jump from the car.

The thoughts became more vicious. *I am going to
destroy him. He's going to pay for what he's done. No
man is going to ever tell me what to do again. Never! I
hate him. I hate all men, even Daddy. He's a man and I
hate him too.* The last thought shocked me into reality.
*No, I don't hate my daddy. You can't make me hate my
daddy.* Swiftly the thoughts changed again. *I ought to kill
you.* My hands were clenched so tightly they hurt. My
thoughts were so loud I was sure Mr. Lee heard them. He
was driving to my home with a look of satisfaction.

When we arrived, I had accepted that I was no longer
the apple in the top of the tree. For the past couple of
weeks, I'd been dangling on the lowest branch close to the
ground. Now I couldn't get any lower. The boys wouldn't

have to reach up to me now; all they had to do was look down. *It's all this man's fault. I may not be able to stop him from using me over and over, but one day I am going to be in control of my own destiny. When that day comes, I dare any man to try and use me again!*

III

13 YEAR OLD JEZEBEL

Deep within, I began experiencing the satisfaction of knowing that somehow I would get even with Mr. Lee. My planned revenge was the only pleasure I had. I rejected God's admonitions that revenge belonged only to Him, that He would repay. I couldn't possibly wait on God. I wanted to be the one to give the orders, instead of taking them. I had taken enough.

In the days and weeks that followed I began to see myself in a different way. I attributed this to the fact that I was now, as Mr. Lee said, grownup. My walk became more provocative. I learned to use body language. My eyes said what I couldn't, and my smile said what I wouldn't. Uncontrolled thoughts directed me, and orders seemingly came from nowhere. Fleshy desires began to grow, desires for clothes, money, power, and for sex, sex on my terms. I knew only one way to handle these desires.

Step by step, I planned my strategy. I had to be pretty in order to attract attention. Nobody wanted a Plain Jane with drab, ordinary clothing. Looking into the mirror only made matters worse. I hated the girl I saw staring back at me. My eyes filled with disgust because my reflection looked dull and unattractive. With a speed and harshness that surprised me, thoughts flooded my mind, *You're ugly, Antoinette. You were always ugly. Nobody is going to want you looking like this. Do something with your face! You need makeup!*

Acceptance of my ugliness motivated me to buy cosmetics to paint my face. However, the suggestions did not stop there. My innocent hairstyle was no longer acceptable. My thoughts became critical of everything about me. This destructive criticism attacked my big, fat braids and the childish bangs on my forehead. This style definitely had to go. I rebelled against Mom so much, she finally gave me permission to do my own hair.

The idea of painting my face progressed to a burning desire, and finally an obsession. I knew I'd never be satisfied until I painted my face. Men always liked a pretty face; therefore, the clothes could come later. I don't remember anyone teaching me to apply makeup. Everyone said I was so adept at it, it must have been an art. No skill had ever come so easily for me.

I wore enough rouge, eyeliner and lipstick to make myself a new face. The finished product stunned me, made me giddy. I had not realized one could create a face from a bottle and compact. In a matter of minutes I'd added four years to my appearance. From then on, my face was regularly purchased at a drug store. The thoughts that I was ugly were gone. I looked good to the whole world, and I knew it. Someone was always available to feed my ego. The recognition built my pride, and I took on a personality resembling Jezebel. My lustful desires were out of control. Mommy couldn't stop me, and Daddy either didn't notice or was too tired to say anything.

Now I needed clothes to complement my new face, to complete the new me. I started wearing tight shorts, halters, pants; suddenly I hated dresses. Whatever I did not have money to buy, I stole. Predictably, Daddy did not like my new clothes. He felt pants had no place in a woman's wardrobe. When he forbade me to wear them, I hid clothes all over the house. I dressed after I went to school. Lying and scheming, I sneaked past Mom each afternoon. Very soon this behavior became uncontrollable.

The day came when I put on a pair of tight shorts, tee shirt, sandals and my new face to walk the streets. With a surge of determination and power, I decided to find a boyfriend. In the six blocks I walked, I drew the guys' attentions like honey draws flies. Deep inside I felt good. My pride was exalted so much I felt I could control the male population. Being attractive had them eating from my hand. I didn't feel ugly or unclean. I was proud! Best of all, I knew one day I'd have my own boyfriend.

After my parade around the neighborhood, I returned home. Mom caught me sneaking into the house. She told me to never put that mess on my face and not to wear those shorts again, but then she left me alone.

Well, Mom, there's no sense in getting yourself upset, because I'm not about to change my appearance for anyone. I felt good mentally telling her off. Although I didn't speak aloud, I talked. No one heard my defiance but me. I'd found a way to be popular, and seen, and I'd continue to do these behaviors if it was the last thing I ever did.

I was just ripe when Mr. Lee came back around the house. With my mind made up, I decided to make the best of a bad situation. Mr. Lee wanted me. I wanted money, clothes and cosmetics. Why not make him pay for them? From now on one hand would wash the other. This time I smiled when Mr. Lee said I was getting prettier every day. Sickened with the old hatred for him, I kept smiling. I told him I needed a few dollars for school and some new clothes.

"Either that, or I tell my daddy." It was blackmail, but so what? It wasn't as bad as what he was doing to me. He gave all I asked willingly. I could tell by his bewildered expression that he knew I had changed. The monster he had created had grown too big to handle, for him or me. I did not stop him from taking me to his room after shopping. I knew what to expect, and I learned to endure.

This time, Mr. Lee wanted to teach me something new. He called it teasing a woman. He began to stimulate my sexual organs. When it was my turn, completely lacking emotion, I did as I was told. A repulsive feeling went through my hands. They felt cold and clammy. Something was definitely wrong. These were the same warm hands I used to write, God's holy hands, my Daddy said. Now they were dirty just like the rest of me. This was not a man and woman teasing each other, but the act of masturbation (as I later learned) being forced upon a child.

While in his room, my mind surrendered to daydreaming. No longer did I plead for my daddy to help. Instead, I entered a world of fantasy. I dreamed of the new boyfriend I'd have, about being rich. I focused my mind on anything that kept me from facing reality. When I could daydream no longer, I silently pled for other ways of escape.

My new escape came in the form of anger. I began to fight. I could see and feel myself screaming, kicking and biting. I threw everything around me. I threw the chair in the corner. I hit Mr. Lee, and if that wasn't enough, I started cursing to let him know I was no longer standing for this. All the hurt came out. I fought so hard I thought I had killed him.

As my body began to relax, I felt slightly dazed from the emotional war. Looking around I realized everything was the same. The chair was still in the corner. Mr. Lee was unhurt. I was still in the same position. It was all inside again. Nothing actually happened. But it seemed so real. Where did the anger and fighting come from? More importantly, where did it go? I hadn't heard profanity like that since I was about eight or nine years old. I hadn't cursed since then. If Daddy knew, I'd be in trouble. Daddy said our sins would find us out. I sure hoped my sins hadn't found me out. Things were bad enough now.

Cursing was nonexistent in our home. I had never heard profanity until I attended school. Now it seemed cursing got the point across better. Cursing represented authority; people paid attention. The words played like a recording in my mind. One day I used the telephone to try my new words. After dialing the operator and hearing her, "May I help you," I let her have all my four-letter words. I did this repeatedly, until one day the operator called me back. She angrily told me she would tell my parents if my activities did not cease.

I was scared. If my parents found out, I'd get the chastisement of my life. Daddy didn't believe in "sparing the rod and spoiling the child." I promised the operator I would never do that again and hung up the phone. I realized I had forgotten to apologize to her. After redialing the number, the operator answered, but I lost my nerve and hung up. Right away the phone rang again. I snatched it up and began to apologize, but no one was on the line. I figured it was a warning from the operator. Shaking from fright, I quickly put the receiver down. Now the curse words were back in my head. Daddy was right; my sins found me out. Just a few hours ago I thought I could endure anything; now I was being dragged under. Maybe if I was more than a little girl, I'd have a chance.

Finally the daytime nightmare with Mr. Lee ended for that day. On the way home Mr. Lee asked me if the boys were beginning to notice me. I could tell he was worried. He even asked me if I had a boyfriend. Anger arose within me again. *Who would want me now, after what you've done to me? I'm of no value to anyone now. I'm not worth anything.* The tongue lashing was all inside. Aloud I gave him the answers he wanted.

"No, I don't have a boyfriend yet." But I didn't tell him I was looking for one either. There was no sense in threatening my money supply. I wasn't about to "cut off my nose to spite my face" as my parents often quoted. My secret was safe within me.

Mr. Lee asked me if I had seen my womanhood yet. I knew what he meant, because he had explained what to look for when he told me about the birds and the bees. He told me this was an important as well as a dangerous time for me, because I could have a baby. "Until then," he said, "you're in no danger. He made me promise to tell him when that time came.

When it did, I thought I was going to die. I had no one to tell me what was happening. We never discussed the facts of life in our home. Since I had tried to tune Mr. Lee out, I could not remember all he had said. I tried to keep my secret as long as I possibly could, but eventually I told my mother. She explained about the changes in my body, and immediately the fear of the unknown left.

As I had promised, I told Mr. Lee when the time came. It was the last time Mr. Lee ever took me to his room. He never told me goodbye or the reason he stopped taking me there.

I was now an old woman at thirteen and a half. Sex forced me to grow up ahead of my time. I had become difficult to handle, and the chance of getting pregnant made me too risky for Mr. Lee.

I was angry and relieved at the same time. I had been used and discarded like an old dishrag, but I was also relieved that this man would never touch me again. For a whole year I had dreamed of this. Why did I feel so lost and insecure?

I felt as if I had been hanging on by a string. I was scared of falling, so I held on very tightly. I didn't even cry when the hurt overwhelmed me. In fact, I became used to it. Now this man was cutting the string, and I had nowhere to fall but down. Once again I thought about the apple in the tree. The poor apple had fallen a long way. It wasn't worth anything to anybody anymore. No matter what it did, it had nothing to lose. No matter how far it went, it would never rise above what it was now. I was that apple.

I returned home with new clothes, money in my pocket, abnormal thoughts, and an education in perverse sexual desires. It was a million years ago that I had wanted to confide in my mother. Only last year? Now it didn't matter. I was still determined not to tell her. My innocence was gone and my personality had changed drastically. I had become cold and callous about many things already. I no longer valued Daddy's high opinion of me. I had lost his high standard, with no means to correct that, so why strive any longer? I was on a roller coaster going downhill for self-destruction. For over a year I had been schooled by a man who possessed perverse sexual habits. What I didn't know was, I now had enough desires to keep me well schooled in the same life without him. I was constantly fed negative thoughts with no one to counteract them. My concept of love was to give my body to anyone who said, "I love you."

IV

THE LUST OF THE FLESH

AND THE PRIDE OF LIFE

"Shut up! Right now, Daddy! Shut up! I hate you! I hate all of you! Leave me alone! It wasn't my fault." Thoughts were having a good time lecturing Daddy. I was hysterical on the outside, and thoughts were cursing and screaming on the inside. I didn't dare let my thoughts speak aloud. They would have told Daddy just how they felt about him. I tried to get away, but Daddy had a firm grip on my arm. He was saying something, but I didn't hear him. I was caught in my own humiliation and hurt.

Getting caught was bad enough. I identified with the woman in the Bible who was caught in the act of adultery. The Bible said, "in the very act." Moses' law said to stone her, and the people were more than willing. But Jesus had mercy on her.

Daddy wasn't having mercy on me. I didn't deserve this. Who would humiliate a fourteen year old girl? After a stern lecture, Daddy let me go. With as much pride as I could muster, I walked to the bedroom to go to bed. My mind wandered as I hid under the covers. I wanted to cry, but that was not allowed. Amid all the hysteria I did not cry. No tears flowed. I couldn't release those emotions.

I knew I was wrong. Sex was wrong without marriage. I had sinned against my own body, and I was only fourteen. This time it wasn't like it had been with Mr. Lee. Nobody forced me. I'd done it willingly. Daddy was only doing the best job he knew. I really deserved to be punished. Facing reality helped me to see clearly. These were the best of times. I knew for certain these were the correct thoughts, and I wanted to do right. I was disgusted with myself and the way I let the guys use me. Although they weren't worth it, I couldn't help myself. If only I could explain that to Daddy. Maybe he could understand.

Poor Mommy. She had caught me with my boyfriend, Bruce. As much as I wanted to say I was sorry, I knew I'd never be able to do so. I was surrounded by an invisible wall of silence that I could not penetrate.

So, just for the record, Daddy, I'm sorry. I'm sorry, Mommy. And if anybody is awake in this bedroom, I'm sorry.

What was wrong with me? I was so much more than the little girl I used to be. I felt like I was divided into different people with moods and desires of their own. There was one little girl who hungered for affection. She desired to hear someone ask her what was wrong. The weight had become too heavy to carry alone. I was so sure that little girl was me, but just as I was about to reach out, others intervened.

The strongest of them was a bitter young woman, aged beyond her years. She was motivated by anger, pride and lust, turning my good intentions to bad ones by unclean thoughts and behaviors. During these times I had no control over my actions or thoughts. She did not allow the real me to come forth until she had completed her deed, which was always disastrous. She wouldn't behave herself. She had no intention of obeying. She wanted to be satisfied. It wasn't me; it was her, yet she was me. I was in a constant state of confusion with no one to identify what

40

was happening in my body or my mind. Unclean thoughts became my thoughts. Harsh words came from my mouth. I now obeyed them more than I obeyed my parents. My actions were responsible for my discipline. The thoughts were in my mind, therefore, it was my thoughts which got me into trouble.

No wonder Daddy said if we just didn't have to think, we'd be all right. Daddy said "we," and he was right. "We" meant "me!" I could no longer blame anyone else for my problems.

It was time I faced reality. I could see me and I could feel me. There was no one else in my body. I did my own thinking! It's just the way I am. I can't help it. I was born this way. Nothing is going to make me better. Everyone might as well get use to me.

Can you hear me, Daddy? Of course you can't hear me! Nobody can. Only I can hear me yelling. I am all alone in this world of silence. I may not be able to say these words out loud, but I can express myself. From now on, that's exactly what I am going to do: express myself. Expression is physical contact. Physical contact is the best medicine for the pain of rejection. Only then did I feel I belonged to someone.

I was caught because I agreed to let Bruce in the house after dark. Daddy and Mommy did not allow him to sit in our house all evening as his parents did. So we agreed he would hide in the backyard until my parents went to bed and then slip in the back door. All went as we planned until Mom caught us, and she told Daddy. Poor Bruce went running as if his life depended on it.

Although Bruce and I continued to see each other, nothing was ever the same between us again. He began to drift away, and there was nothing I could do to stop it. Soon he stopped coming around at all. I heard he had another girl. She was very pretty and wore no makeup.

My heart felt as if it had turned to stone. All that I had was taken the first time, and I was thrown away.

This time, I gave all that I had, willingly, and I was still thrown away. Once rejected! Twice rejected! Three times, Antoinette, and you're out!

The hurt went deep. Two men threw me away. Not one, but two. What was wrong with me? I was no longer ugly. I'd seen to that. Why didn't anything work? I had so many unanswered questions, but they did not remain unanswered long. My thoughts would tell me what to do. When Thoughts had something to say, I could not silence them.

Thoughts said, *I am too soft. I let my guard down. By letting my feelings get in the way, I exposed myself to man. It is a sign of weakness. This must never happen again. Never again am I to do that.*

Thoughts made me see myself more clearly, They opened my eyes. What a relief to know it wasn't my fault. Thoughts were right. I needed Thoughts. Without them I was nothing. From then on I resolved to obey Thoughts even if I had to destroy myself.

My list of problems expanded rather than diminished. My "I don't care" attitude brought me to the point that I was in dangerous situations with no regard for the outcome. I gave into lustful desires and thoughts time and again. My parents lost all control of me. I went to church only because I had to. I hated school and routinely played hookey. My only interest was to find someone with whom I could release my pent-up desires.

Our house soon became a war zone as my mother and I began to fight. My mouth was terrible; I just came short of cursing. Many times Mommy had to hit me in the mouth to shut me up. This only made things worse. I was already hurt. I didn't need more. I wasn't raised to cuss and couldn't understand how the horrible language came out of my mouth. But it was my mouth, therefore, it had to be me.

My body became as filthy as my mouth. At times I could not remember when I had taken a complete bath. My teeth began to suffer. Once strong, pretty and white, they now were plagued with cavities. Mom tried everything to make me clean up. She tried embarrassing me. She said I was nasty and dirty, and she was right. I deserved it; I knew it. She wasn't the only one who called me dirty. My body proved it. The teachers in school began to complain. Finally my peers began to tease me.

I felt so bad. I'd cry on the inside, but nobody could hear or see me. For the next few days I'd work hard to keep my body clean. It worked sometimes, however, every time I used the soap and water a repulsive feeling resulted. I couldn't handle it, so I stopped trying again. Unclean!

When the teachers threatened to send me home, Mom forced me to wash. Couldn't she see something was restraining me? I felt the weight of it holding me down.

I wanted people to leave me alone. I didn't want to be bothered, but my body gave off an entirely different reaction. The same uncontrollable desires began to flame up inside me again. A fire was going through my loins. At the same time my thoughts touted a hatred for men, my body cried out Lust!

Automatically, as if guided by a mind of their own, my hands remembered another time. Thus began a habit of masturbation. It took over as if motivated by some unseen force. Mr. Lee was right about one thing. It was teasing; my body was teasing me. It was crying for satisfaction, and she would receive it at all costs. The hands were quick and ready. The mind followed the hands. They were in one accord with each other. Whatever the hands said to do, the mind totally agreed. I had no will or emotion to fight it. Masturbation carried me along like a tidal wave. At last the burning desire stopped. The tense feeling left, and my body could relax. Totally in control again, I was tired and disgusted. I felt ashamed.

A mass of confusion, I hungered for love and attention, but could not receive it. I wanted to be held, yet the fear of being rejected kept me at a distance. There were light days when my mind was at peace. I was happy to be alive. When the dark days arrived, I was miserable. I knew exactly when those times were approaching. My body sent its warning signals. Depression preceded insecurity and I finally was left feeling I would never amount to anything.

The depressions were followed by periods of exaltation. My ego had to be boosted. I had to be seen and recognized for who I was. I was a pretty girl, and no one dare tell me otherwise. The old me was put away. All the flaws and imperfections were hidden. Perfection must come forth. Everything in its proper place. Anything short of it was not tolerated. First I applied the paint, then the careful selection of a revealing outfit, something that attracted attention.

Only when I was proud of how I looked could I leave the house. I walked the streets looking for boyfriends. Soon I picked up quite a reputation. I needed to be seen, and I was. I always told myself that I wouldn't do anything, that I just wanted to hear someone tell me I looked good. However, what began as a parade around the block, became much more. After losing control and the proud, lustful desires were satisfied, I was left in a pitiful state. I wondered how I could have done such things. Just when I needed an answer, Thoughts deserted me. I was forced to face the deeds done in my body. I couldn't talk to anyone; I was again closed in my own world. Without Thoughts, I had no direction, no plans, no desire to do anything. I lacked motivation. I was slowly becoming dependent upon Thoughts.

"Nettie, you have a letter in the mail." I couldn't think of anyone who would write to me, but looking at the return address, I immediately knew the letter was from Mr. Lee.

Mr. Lee had left New York to return to his hometown for his remaining years. He had written to see how I was doing, and sent me a couple of dollars to purchase things I needed. That only made me angry; he was just trying to soothe his conscience. He could never pay me enough money. Changing my mind, I sat down and wrote him a letter. I let him know he had not sent me enough money, that I needed more. I wanted new clothes, makeup, and sundries. Either he send the money or I tell my father what he did to me. With complete satisfaction, I put the letter in the mail. I had no doubt the money would be mailed. And it was, time and time again. Without doubts about what I was doing, but I felt no remorse. I was now the cat, and he was the helpless canary.

Little by little I was acquiring a new identity. Even my name became a thing of the past. I was called Toni and loved it. Soon there would be none of the old me left. It was very important that I put all that old Antoinette behind me.

Although I was pleased with the new me, there was still room for improvement. Something about my appearance was not quite right. My hair did nothing to complement the new me. Hatred for my own hair began to take root. I noticed other girls' hair and coveted what they had. My own hair was actually good enough, but I could not see that. Desire for someone else's hair blinded me to my own. The texture was wrong. It wasn't long or thick enough. I thought longer, prettier hair would make a big difference in my appearance. I needed hair that bounced with I walked, so the guys would have to notice me. No one would ignore me then.

Where could I get hair like that overnight? A woman in our church wore a wig. I heard her tell my mother that it was very expensive, because it was custom made. Custom made or not, I could never afford a wig. My own hair would just have to do. I tried putting the thought of wigs and hairpieces out of my mind, but as hard as I tried, I was no longer satisfied with my own hair. I could not rest; this desire consumed my every waking hour. I resolved I'd one day find a way to fulfill this desire, as I had with everything else in my life.

Soon I received another letter in the mail, but this one came from an inmate in the county jail. A friend there showed my picture to an inmate named Everett, who wrote me a letter. I quickly wrote him back. Through correspondence, we became acquainted, and in time, I became the girlfriend of a prisoner I had never seen.

The day came when Everett was released from prison. I waited with anticipation to meet my new boyfriend in person. After our introduction, Everett and I began seeing each other every chance we had. We began conducting ourselves as if we were married, although we were without one important document, the marriage license.

One morning I awoke so sick I could barely get out of bed. At first I thought I had a stomach virus, but when it lasted longer than expected, I began to worry. Finally, I missed my monthly cycle, and fearfully began to pray. I made all sorts of promises to God, if He would just help me out of this trouble I'd created.

But I'd already had my chance and neglected to take it. Now I was faced with the usual problems of unwed pregnant teens. I thought about marriage, and my parents, abortion. I did not want to get married. I could not tell my parents, and abortion was out of the question.

What would other people say? My daddy was a preacher of the gospel. I was a shame and a disgrace, and I knew it. With no answers of my own, I needed Mom and Dad as never before, but I could not talk to them. Someone else would have to tell my parents.

I no longer cared about my appearance. Pride meant nothing now, and lust had put me in serious trouble. Eventually my secret showed. The moment I stepped into the house that day, I was aware that Mom knew. She was hurt; I could hear it in her voice. Her only instruction was to finish my school term, and we would take care of the rest later. She would inform Daddy.

Going into my room, I sought the only escape I knew. Although I knew my body required more rest now, I was using sleep as a way to escape the unbearable pressure. Whatever I could not, or did not want to face, I covered with sleep.

The sound of my father coming home awakened me. My mom must have told him. I was afraid to go into the living room to face him, but I could not hide forever. With as much courage as I could gather, I faced Daddy. The expected thunder did not occur, in fact, he did not even ask me why. I heard nothing from him.

I could take anything but his silence. Silence had already closed upon me from all sides, and now my daddy had also. His rejection was confirmed by Thoughts which tormented my mind. This rejection impacted me harder than any previous hurt. This was worse than any rejection from a boyfriend.

Once rejected! Twice rejected! Three times and you're out, Antoinette! My own thoughts were laughing at me. They were right; I had gone down for the third time. A beating would have been better than this. Having no answers of my own, I could not face what had just happened.

I was so tired; sleep was a welcome relief. It became a pleasure. When Sleep manifested, I became inactive. Soon I became its slave. The habit was uncontrollable.

Mom began to accuse me of laziness, which angered me.

I'm not lazy. I was never lazy. I'm just tired.

47

I wished to say everything aloud. Maybe if I could express myself, someone would understand. Try as I might, there was only a silent conversation for me.

Everett, Mom and Dad began to make marriage plans for me. I did not want to get married, but I let them plan. I kept hoping the marriage would never take place. I did not know this man, and I was afraid of getting married. Fear of the unknown held a strong grip on me.

A few weeks before the marriage was to take place, I received another letter. Postmarked from the county jail, I knew immediately Everett was back in jail. Never have I felt such release. Mom and Dad weren't pleased, but they never made me feel bad. I think they knew I could not bear any more.

I had only one more request of God. Like Absalom and his father David, I wanted my daddy to speak to me again. If God would do that for me, I would try my best to behave myself.

V

YOU'RE A STUPID AND LAZY GIRL

"Congratulations, Antoinette. You have a 8 1/2 pound baby boy." At the age of sixteen, I was a mother. My first thoughts were for my baby. I did not know what to do with him. I had no means of support. His father was in prison. I was a high school dropout with no job training. With all the problems I had, one more was added to the list. I was now responsible for another generation to lay claim to the welfare system.

During my ten days in the hospital I did some soul searching. Able to see and think clearly, I was ready for a change. I left the hospital with the intention of improving my relations with my family. I did not know what the future held for me, but anything had to be better than the past.

My brothers and sisters gave me a big welcome when I returned home. But a better surprise was in store. My dad spoke to me. Not only did he speak, but love and concern were in his voice. I wanted to tell Daddy that I loved him, but didn't know how. I felt he had the same desire, but he too remained silent. I reached up and shyly kissed him on the cheek. He smiled. That action spoke louder than words. Everything was all right in my world.

Things went well for me for many months. I had a few close calls with boyfriends, but nothing that pulled me back. I still tried my best to look attractive, but the uncontrollable desire for recognition had lost its stronghold. I knew my parents did not appreciate the makeup, so I toned it down to almost nothing. I stopped wearing it to church, in which I became active again. Now my aim was to make up for some of the hurt I had caused. I had no trouble making things right with Mom. She had a true mother's heart. I still wanted my father to be proud of me, and he was. The old Antoinette was back, and it felt good to be myself again.

Time moved swiftly. My baby, born in December, was becoming more of a handful by September. September meant one thing to me: school. I wanted to complete my education, but I knew Mom's viewpoint on the subject and dared not ask. She was right. The baby was my responsibility. I still did not stop hoping that Mom would change her mind and take care of him for me, while I completed school. I clung to that ray of hope like a drowning person clings to a lifeguard.

Each passing hour brought the opening of school closer. Still Mom said no word about watching the baby for me. I was on pins and needles while school preparations were being made in our home. My expectations grew. One day I noticed a sadness I had not experienced for a long time. It was replaced by discouragement, and then impatience. Impatience led to anger, and I began to snap at everyone, including the baby. As the moods changed, I could see the old behavior patterns coming forth.

I tried to block them by focusing my mind on good things. Instead, I lost ground. The more I tried to think positively, the more the negative I became. Pressure began to build, which I found difficult to control. The struggle was familiar, but why? It was definitely my body, but strange emotions were laying claim to it. A sudden twist in behavior fought to gain control. I was being forced into the background, and I no longer had the power or authority to tell the intruder he could not take what was mine. I could only stand back and let the thieves steal and destroy what I had regained in the past nine months.

There seemed to be so many of me. My entire body was split into different personalities. Each had its own thing to do and say. In the midst of this confusion, I had no control. No one understood how I was fine one day and completely the opposite the next. I needed help or I would be destroyed.

The first day of school arrived, and everyone marched off except me. I always enjoyed learning, but now the opportunity was taken away. Deep down I knew it wasn't Mom's fault, but someone had to shoulder the blame. I became angry at everyone. My baby was at fault! Mom was at fault! I wanted to cry but couldn't. I was a well that had dried up. Something or someone was restraining me from my true emotions.

I had been doing so well, exhibiting normal behavior. I believed the old Antoinette was back, but the bad Thoughts and desires were only quiet for awhile. When I thought everything was fine, they moved in and turned my world upside down again. They controlled me; they played with my emotions. Having no mercy, they did as they desired, and I reaped the destruction.

No longer were there only two or three, but many. Lustful desires and bad thoughts grouped together for reinforcement. Together we were dragged down into a cesspool of filth. The uncontrollable desire for sleep returned, but supervising a baby did not allow me to sleep when I wanted. Desires did not care; sleep overwhelmed me anyway. I made the baby lie down and sleep with me. If he did not sleep, I became angry.

I lost all motivation to accomplish any chores. Diapers were left in the pail unwashed. The baby was not kept clean. Mom said I was lazy; I said I was tired. I cursed Mom in my mind, and Thoughts enjoyed it. Only I heard the filthy words. I lost all desire to attend church, but I went because Daddy was a firm believer in "as for me and my house, we shall serve the Lord."

Even in church I became distracted. Noticing one of my girlfriends reading a magazine, I asked her to share it. She handed me a romance magazine. Immediately, I fell in love. On Sundays I sat in church reading magazines.

Reading romances opened a new distraction for me. Until then, the most influential book I'd read was the Bible. At an early age God had shaped my mind through the set of Bible stories given to us when we were children. In many hours of joyful reading, the Biblical people came alive for me. I became acquainted with Jesus Christ and the patriarchs. The writers of the Bible left such an impression on me, that I began to write plays and poetry as early as eleven and twelve years old. Although my parents did not read well, they knew the importance of good reading habits. For my tenth birthday I was given a new set of *World Book Encyclopedias*, which I absorbed almost as much as the Bible.

Lustful desire, however, changed my reading habits also. I had found a new escape. Reading romance magazines focused my mind on adultery, fornication, divorce, romance and depravity. My head spun with secrets, confessions and sex. I decided to one day be a writer of romance novels.

"Nettie, Mr. Lee died!" My emotion was not grief. Now I would not have to kill him, but I wanted my past to be as dead as Mr. Lee. Standing in front of the mirror, I had a serious conversation. I told self I wanted it all blocked out of my mind. The years I was twelve and thirteen were not to be part of my memory. I even vowed to block out anything that was too big to handle, and I did.

Soon I felt the shortage of money. My desires were not diminishing and welfare certainly was not enough. I began to seek a job after my neighbor volunteered to care for my baby during school hours. My sisters volunteered to help after school.

The job lasted one day. I did not like working, and my baby sitter refused to keep a spoiled baby. I should have been disappointed, instead, I was relieved. I could not argue with Mom now when she said I was lazy. Laziness had hold of me, and depression set in. My thoughts began to torment me again, and I could not follow my own directions.

I am stupid and lazy. Without an education I will never amount to anything. I must do what I do best. Fix myself up! Look at me; I've let myself go. I should have known better. My baby needs a father. I'll get myself a husband. Anybody will do, as long as I get one.

VI

ADULTERY

The Four Tops' hit single blared from the radio. They sounded good as I rode in the open convertible. I had found a husband, but he wasn't mine. He belonged to someone else in the neighborhood. I did not care that Sam had a wife, nor did I care if she knew I was seeing him. At sixteen, I was interested in only one thing, to have a good time.

The past was finally behind me. I could express myself now. I didn't know why I had chosen Sam, because I didn't like him much. What drove me to him was not love. Maybe it was his car. Maybe it was his spending money. Whatever the reason, he was mine for a time. I felt comfortable with this affair. I knew I was not going to be rejected this time. When I tired of this one, I'd get rid of him and go on to the next one.

When I met Sam's wife, I felt sorry for her. Under different circumstances, I could have liked her. I often wondered how she could let any man use her the way Sam did. She stayed home. She cleaned and cooked for a man who ran around on her. Feeling contempt for her dedication, I decided she wasn't a wife, but a slave. When I lost interest in Sam, I dropped him.

I knew better, but I committed adultery over and over again. Lustful desires for someone else's husband kept getting the best of me. "Thou shalt not" was not in my vocabulary. Desires said yes, and so I did. The adulterous relationships continued into my adult years. Some I dated, to others I just listened. Each had an excuse for cheating. I was not the only adulteress, but I lent a sympathetic ear. I took interest in their jobs which I knew nothing about. Many hours were spent talking and encouraging these men.

Most of the time I had little or no regret. The wife was the husband's problem, not mine. He had to take care of her and keep her out of the picture. Any time I decided to size up the competition, I'd purposely go to the same party with a group of friends. My pride loved to watch the husband squirm while I played cat and mouse. I was gloating on the inside, but calm on the outside. The experience with Mr. Lee had schooled me well, but that was in my forgotten past. Making sure I looked good, I waited for the husband to take his wife home and leave her.

The phone call always followed, but I never gave my total self. That meant trouble. Any woman who fell in love with a married man had my sympathy. I could not be that stupid. Attachments and adultery won't mix.

Later, dating married men became a convenience. I rejected all authority from men. He was not my husband, therefore he could not tell me what to do. Once demands were made, it was time for me to move on. Adultery was a secret I hardly guarded. It was not my concern if the husband was not ready to announce he was having an extra-marital affair. If some wives were willing to fight for what was theirs, I moved on. Some wives didn't care as long as they received the paycheck. Fine with me. Others had wives who were committing adultery themselves. Bravo! I gave this poor unfortunate husband my compassion and time. Together we found a way to get even.

I met men who were bored with home life and looking for excitement. They were willing to risk the price of exposure; gifts and excuses usually brought forgiveness from their wives. Some husbands had wives who had let themselves go. Some husbands complained that their houses were dirty and dinner was never on time. I knew the right words to boost deflated egos. Others had wives who were too inhibited, afraid to let go. Some wives were too wrapped up in their children and jobs. The husbands were left lonely and reaching for companionship. One husband had a church-going wife, who because of her church duties, had pushed her husband into the background. I was the background.

Others just wanted to talk about their problems, such as the wife-beater, who was always sorry afterwards. One just could not be faithful. He had no complaints; he loved his wife, but he was driven by lust and adultery. He and other men were reared with the idea that infidelity was part of their manhood. They weren't "men" unless they had more than one woman. We all had one thing in common, adultery.

I was convinced I wasn't hurting anyone. It was my body and I did with it as I desired. Problems in the home were not my concern. The marriage must have been in trouble anyway, or I would not have been in the picture. I refused to accept the responsibility, but when the heat was on, I just walked away.

Although I made myself available, I never had to ask a husband out. Getting a date with a married man was usually easier than a single man. We laughed together at the ridiculous excuses we managed to offer, the time he almost was caught, all his narrow escapes.

I met one man who claimed to be single. He was foolish enough to give me his home phone number, and I never considered not using it to my advantage. I laughed at the many times I called and his wife answered. Knowing she was not his sister, I'd tell her what I wanted without giving my name. I never worried about the consequences.

He got what he deserved. I was not the first and I would not be the last.

I met many couples who had no desire to hide adultery. Most bragged of at least one extra-marital affair. Others entered into their marriage with infidelity as the unspoken agreement. Marriage was seldom seen as a sacred institution. We laughed at husband and wife swapping, and ignored the damage that sex therapists were doing to the sanctity of the marriage bed.

My parents became sick of my behavior. Home was not a place I could do as I pleased. I needed to move out, but that required money, which meant a job. I had no intentions of working. I had tried welfare, but the welfare office informed me I was too young to live on my own with a baby. They insisted I wait one more year.

I had no time to wait. The only alternative was to get a husband of my own. All he had to do was provide the material needs and get me out of my parents' house.

Noticing a new guy in the neighborhood who knew nothing about me, I realized he was the one to marry. He looked the right age; he had a job and was good-looking. Soon we were dating like old friends. I introduced him to my family. His church background pleased my parents, and we were soon engaged.

We were fighting even before we married, but we assumed sex would take care of the fighting. In the middle of our wedding plans, I discovered I was pregnant again. Tim was proud and assured me he would not back out now.

With all the problems I had, I settled down during our courtship. I lost all interest in other men, and my lifestyle changed considerably. Even my thinking was different. I really wanted to get married, although I was unsure about love. I desired to be the faithful wife who stayed home and kept house while her husband worked. My life began a period of normalcy, and I wanted to keep it that way. With all the odds against us, this marriage was going to work. Antoinette was her old self again.

My wedding day fulfilled two secret desires I had harbored for a long time. One was a new husband; the other was an eighteen inch hairpiece. Toni finally had the hair and the man she desired.

Only one obstacle occurred. My soon-to-be husband lost his job. Although we had no extra finances, I refused to postpone the wedding. Everything would go as planned.

The day of the wedding, I had the best wedding ring five dollars could buy. After the wedding, we went to the Social Service Department to apply for welfare, only until Tim got another job. What a honeymoon!

VII

I DO TAKE THIS MAN...

"Toni, please don't have me locked up again. I can't hack this jail. Please, Toni."

I almost felt sorry for my husband. Just as I was about to take a step toward him, the police officer spoke.

"We're sorry, sir, but this case is out of your wife's hand. It's a case against the city. Mrs., you may go now."

I refused to accept blame for having Tim locked up. I tried to warn him over and over. I should have known I was marrying a wife-beater. The warning signs were all there. I had been in such a hurry to leave home that I'd ignored all the signals. As I walked from the police precinct, I couldn't help wondering how I came to this point..

Soon after we were married, Tim was offered a decent job, and we managed to get off welfare, at least for a few months. When Tim lost that one, we trotted back to the Social Service Department. I began to feel that poverty was my middle name. It was easy to slip into the pattern all over again, since I had been dependent upon welfare from childhood. I knew what it was to live from month to month, depending on a grant from Services.

In spite of the struggles and not much money, I enjoyed being married. I was free to run the household as I saw fit. Being a married woman not only helped me face responsibility, it also brought me much closer to my parents. Being on good terms with them helped me appreciate what they had been trying to teach me all along. Finally the past was buried and the hurts behind me.

At age 73, Dad's health began to deteriorate. In all our years we had never known him to have even a headache. Just before Christmas Dad was rushed to the hospital with a stroke caused by high blood pressure. He never regained consciousness. Eight days later, on Christmas morning, the same day he was born, he died. Mom broke down at the funeral. Normally I would have cried, but I could not. I only felt bad for Mom and uncomfortable. Glad we were on peaceful terms when it happened, I was extremely grateful that all the old hurts were behind us. I knew my father would rest in peace with God. Two weeks after my father's funeral, and one week after the new year, I gave birth to my second son.

I began to notice signs of restlessness in Tim. Just as I feared, he was tired of married life. I felt he wanted a wife and family, but also wanted to hang out with the guys. Very seldom did he think about going to work. Welfare took care of all our expenses, so Tim could take his time looking for a job. When he managed to get one, it never lasted more than a few months at the most.

Tim and I began to fight more bitterly and frequently. He always apologized, and I accepted his apologies, but I limped around with sunglasses to hide the bruises afterward. My stories about walking into furniture did not fool anyone, but I was too ashamed to tell anyone that my husband was beating me. I wanted everyone to think my marriage was a success. To leave him and return home would be an admission of failure. My children needed their father, so I covered for him, on the outside. Inside, I knew one day he'd pay for what he did to me. Until that time, I fought back. Tim was left with permanent scars where my fingers had dug into his flesh. I threw anything I could reach at him during our fights. The children were frightened; the neighbors heard, but I was beyond caring during the fight. I was defending myself. I began to curse along with Tim. My language became as bad as his. I promised myself over and over that I would not curse, but the words just slipped out.

I had another mouth problem; I just couldn't shut up in an argument. Sometimes I initiated the arguments, which I regretted. Knowing that if I would just shut up, sometimes our arguments would not continue, did not give me control of the problem. Even while Tim had his hand around my throat telling me to shut up, I was still arguing and cursing. I had to have the last word. And I almost did. In my verbal abuse, I always reminded him of our last struggle, even if it was a year before. All my anger and hurt poured out of me.

Tim continued to run the streets. What began as a weekend activity, quickly spilled into the middle of the week also. I began to notice lipstick and perfume on his clothes. Those were a result of close dancing in the bars, he said. In order to pacify me, Tim agreed to take me to his hangout.

We went to a bar. Since I did not drink, he ordered a coke on the rocks for me. Sitting there, I sensed a fear around me. I remembered my father saying bars were the devil's territory. Was I waiting for Satan to make an appearance? If he did, I did not recognize him, and I soon stopped looking for him.

The bar was crowded. When Tim's friends began to arrive about midnight, one of his buddies asked Tim why he was in the streets if he had a wife at home. I knew what he meant. Tim was cheating on me, but I had no proof. That explained his nights out and his shortage of money. Part of me was hoping it was true, so I could have an excuse to do my thing. The other part of me hoped it wasn't true, because his infidelity put me in the same category as the wife who could not keep her husband home.

I enjoyed my night on the town. It was a night I would not soon forget. I held its memory close to me, because I felt I was coming back. After that night, I felt myself becoming more and more discontented with just being a housewife. I became angry with my husband. He could just drop family responsibilities and walk off; I was a woman tied down. I began to resent my position in life and in the home. I could easily carry on the role of mother during the day and at night, slip into the role of single, carefree woman.

Tim began to stay away later and later. Finally, he was gone all night. He admitted he was having an affair. Now the shoe was on the other foot. I was the wife, and one of my closest girlfriends was the other woman. She was someone I had confided in. She had all the inside information she needed to keep my husband satisfied. She knew about our fights and the reasons for them. She knew his dislikes, interests, and my weaknesses. She was the one who now encouraged my husband and boosted his deflated ego.

The hurt was beyond words. Tim was mine, and no other woman had the right to what was mine, especially not my so-called friend. I begged, cried, pleaded, to no avail. I spent sleepless nights alone. My mind played tricks on me. Imagining where my husband was, I could see her in his arms over and over. The ticking of the clock informed me how slowly time was moving. My husband had all night with her, and I had all night alone. I tried to sleep on the couch, in the bed, sometimes on the floor. I stared blankly at the TV, and then finally at a blank screen in the early morning hours. As I watched the sun rise, I listened for his footsteps to grace the apartment hallway.

Once home, I knew better than to fight. Taking a different approach, I remained calm. I tried to extend love and patience to him. I thought if I could outdo the other woman, I would be able to hold onto my marriage. When I could hold on no longer, I gave him an ultimatum. It was either her or me.

He chose both. He said he loved me, but could not give her up. The choice was now mine. One night, as I lay on the floor in front of the door waiting for Tim to come home, I felt the door opening against my body about 4 A.M. I was shivering from the cold draft blowing beneath the doorsill. I tried one last time to get my husband to come to his senses. He didn't, but I did. I had been making a fool of myself because this man did not love me enough to be faithful.

How could I have been so stupid? I had never let a man use me like this. What had happened to me? Somewhere I had lost my identity! I wasn't something to be rejected and discarded like an old dishrag! I was a woman! It was about time I acted like one. I began to slowly update my wardrobe. I bought new wigs and hairpieces. I knew I was attractive and would have no trouble finding what I wanted. I no longer wanted Tim, but he wouldn't go anywhere without a fight. By the time I was finished he would be glad to leave.

I learned how to drink. I tried smoking, but quickly gave it up. Alcohol would do. It made me bold, and it gave me courage to go into bars. The roles were reversed. When Tim realized I was not sitting home, he began to take notice. At some time, he dropped his girlfriend, but I considered his action too late. I would not forget and had no forgiveness in me. Turning to alcohol, men, and parties, I was on my way to proving that a woman can do better. Tim eventually turned to drugs.

The fights intensified. Once in a while Time asked me out and I agreed, but at some time in the evening we always began to fight. I became tired of being abused and resorted to calling the police. They were not much help.

Their solutions amounted to walking or driving Tim around the block to give him a chance to cool.

Tim's weight dropped from his drug use. I hated drugs, and I hated what Tim allowed heroin to do to him and our home. Drugs took us deeper into poverty than ever. Finally our rent had to be vouchered by Social Services. We did not see the money; it went directly to the landlord. That became a blessing in disguise. At least I could count on a roof over our heads.

Tim became a slave to the heroin needle. Between his addiction and jealousy, and my uncontrollable tongue, our fights were frightening. I was running scared. I decided to take the advice of the police officers.

During the next fight, the heel of Tim's shoe chipped my hip bone. The pain was excruciating. I called the police, but Tim managed to convince them I was all right.

"It was just a little family misunderstanding," he told them.

Later in the night I went to the emergency room, alone, to get a pain killer. The emergency room staff called the police. These officers were kind and sympathetic. They explained that the previous officers had not known I was hurt, and explained how I could obtain an order of protection from the courts, first thing in the morning.

That was fine for tomorrow, but what about tonight? I had no protection. I was beyond caring what happened to me or Tim any longer. I just knew no man was going to beat me again. I wasn't a child. I was a woman! Returning home, I went into the kitchen and took a knife from the kitchen drawer. I slept with the knife under my pillow all night. If Tim had made a wrong move, it would have been his last. Instead, sorry for his actions, he just apologized.

The next morning I made my way into family court. The judge was on my side. My protection meant if Tim abused me verbally or otherwise, I was to call the police, and they would lock him up immediately. That was all I needed. That court-ordered paper spelled my freedom. I could speak my peace and not be beaten.

Sometimes I did not see my husband for days. He was somewhere trying to kick drugs cold turkey. Anything he did was fine with me as long as he was out of my way. His attempts were short-lived. The craving for drugs soon reoccurred. One shot of heroin and Tim was right back to his habit.

One morning I tried to get into the bathroom and found Tim slumped over the toilet. At first I thought he was dead, and I ran. When I returned, he was all right. He had just taken a shot of heroin and was waiting for the drug to take effect. Hatred arose in me. He had a problem, but it was none of my concern. I couldn't help him. I just wanted him out of my life so I could continue to do my thing.

Our roles were reversed. It didn't bother me that my husband caught me stepping from my boyfriend's car one night. When I was dropped off in the neighborhood, it didn't bother me that Tim was home waiting for me. One morning at 4 o'clock, he could wait no longer. Fearing that something must have happened to me, he left the apartment to find me. He found the shoe was on the other foot now. It was his wife who was committing adultery.

I could see emotions going through his eyes. First, unbelief, then hurt, and anger. As he reached to grab my arm, I threatened to get back into the car and never return. For the first time, I saw Tim back down. He was defeated and he knew it. I guess he realized he could not beat love or faithfulness into me. He began to beg. He wanted forgiveness and reconciliation.

I did not. I was tired of married life, especially the housewife routine. All I wanted was my freedom. Someone had to be the loser, and as far as I was concerned, it was not going to be me.

I cut Tim down repeatedly. For his one known affair, I made him pay many times. In every affair or argument I had, I reminded him of his errors. When the fights began again, I ran to the law for protection. He was locked up more than once. When he was free from wife abuse, drug-related incidents locked him up again. I constantly reminded him that he was weak and I could do better. I knew his dependency on heroin had impaired his mental and physical abilities, but I wanted him out of my way. I now wore the pants in the family. I could and would take care of the household on my own.

"Toni, I can't hack this jail!" Tim was telling the truth. As I left the precinct, I could still hear him pleading. I walked on. His body would go through withdrawal in the city jail. To officers and wardens he was just another junkie and wife-abuser.

I was granted a court order to bar Tim from our home indefinitely, due to his admission to drugs, and our fights. I had achieved what I wanted. We were married in 1966 for better or worse. In 1970 the worse brought separation and divorce. Tim left New York, and I was given custody of my children.

Free at last. It was a dream come true. I was my own boss and I didn't have to give account to anyone. I forgot one thing. My father had taught, "daughter, one day your sins will find you out."

VIII

MENTALLY DEPRESSED

"Are you Antoinette Cannaday?"

Meekly I answered "yes" to the police officer. I showed no visible signs of anger, although I had just been in a fight.

"Antoinette, you have the right to remain silent. If you give up the right to remain silent, anything you say, can, and will be used against you in a court of law. Do you understand what I just said to you?"

"Yes sir, I do. Won't you please come in and have a seat?"

The officers followed my invitation and entered my living room. I sat opposite them and put my head in my hands not knowing what to expect.

"Did you have a fight with the woman downstairs?"

"Yes sir, I did."

"What did you hit her with?"

"My hands, sir."

"Your hands did that? She looks like you used some sort of weapon on her. She's mighty banged up. Right now she's unconscious. We're sorry, Antoinette, but we have to place you under arrest."

"You mean, you're taking me to jail?"

"Yes ma'am, we're sorry. We understand you have children. Is there anyone you can call to take care of them?"

"Yes sir. I'll call my mother."

After arrangements were made for my children, and my needs were taken care of, the police officers took me downstairs. One of the officers started to handcuff me, but changed his mind. I was told if my neighbor regained consciousness, it was a possibility I would be released on my own recognizance that night.

When we arrived at the station, I was fingerprinted and charged with a Class D felony. If my neighbor, who was also my friend, did not recover, the charge would become more serious. After being placed in a cell, I had more time to think about how I had gotten into this trouble.

I had gone to my friend's apartment to ask her why she betrayed my confidence. She jumped me. I began to swing with all my might. Even after she was down, I swung. I felt someone pushing me and yelling to get upstairs into my apartment. By then it was all over. I never meant to get angry, but I couldn't help it. Anger, expressed through my words at first, spread through my body like heat. It took control of my hands and mind. All I could do was fight. I was left with the results.

Dad had said, "get angry, but sin not." This must be what he meant. This was sin. I was in serious trouble. Suppose this woman did not regain consciousness? I would be imprisoned for many years. I wished to turn the clock back. Who will take care of my babies? Mom won't. All this thinking burdened my mind; I needed to relax.

I didn't know where my personal possessions were, but I had to find them to take my medication. Anytime I had pain, the doctors gave me a prescription for painkillers. I had pain now, not physical, but pain. The emotional pain depressed me. I needed to escape. When I did not want to face reality, I popped one of the painkillers. Many times they were lifesavers, like right now. I couldn't sit in this jail cell all night without something to make it bearable, but

I had to convince the warden I was feeling discomfort to get them.

"Yes, Antoinette, what do you want?"

"I have medication in my pocketbook for pain, and I need to take it now. I'm under a doctor's care. You can check the bottle. It's on the label."

As she went for verification, I had no doubt that I would get my pills. I always managed to get medication when I needed it. Soon the warden returned with my pills in hand. She handed me one and went to get a cup of water. I reached into my blouse for another pill I kept on hand. As the pills slipped down my throat, I smiled anticipating the mellow high soon to follow. It was only a temporary relief, about four hours, but I could sleep after that.

As the pills took effect, I escaped into my own world of unreality. I had no problems. My children were fine. Why worry about anything? Tomorrow I would be out of jail and out of trouble. Even this place did not look bad. The warden returned to check on me. I told her I felt fine, and I did. If only she knew how good I felt! I couldn't help giggling to myself.

The night ended sooner than I expected. The warden informed me I would be going to court this morning, and she did not expect to see me back here again. She wished me all the best.

The ride to court was filled with mixed emotions. I was not under the effect of the pills and no longer angry. I had to face the judge soberly.

Inside the back of the court room, I was held in the holding pen for prisoners waiting to appear before the judge. I found my predicament unbelievable. Because of my momentary outburst, I had almost killed my neighbor. If she did not regain consciousness, I would be facing a murder charge.

At two o'clock I was given a court-appointed attorney. Once my name was called, my attorney began my defense before the judge.

"Your honor, my client admits she did have a fight, and she is pleading for the mercy of the court. She has never been in any trouble before. I do not believe it would be beneficial for her to be locked away from society. As a single parent, she is solely responsible for the welfare of her children. Her neighbor has regained consciousness and does not desire to press charges. We are asking that all charges against her be dropped, and that she be released on her own recognizance and returned to her family."

After his summation, I waited in front of the court for the judge to pass sentence upon me.

"Antoinette, I hope you realize the seriousness of this charge. What you did could cause you to spend up to a minimum of one year in prison. Had the injury you inflicted on your neighbor been of a more serious nature, you would now be faced with a more serious charge than that of misdemeanor. I do not understand how you got into this trouble in the first place. You do not appear to be the type of young lady involved in these situations. If you don't get into trouble again within the next six months, upon your next appearance, the courts will then seal this case. You will have no record. I expect to see you before this court again in six months. If you do not appear a warrant will be issued for your arrest."

"Your neighbor does not desire to press charges, therefore, I am releasing you on your own recognizance. However, I am imposing a hundred dollar fine as a stipulation to your release, to be paid immediately. Do you have the money?"

My boyfriend, Jay, stepped forward with the hundred dollars.

"Okay, you may go now."

Just as I was about to leave, the judge called me again.

"Antoinette, your outcome has been good. They don't all end this way. Go home and contribute to society." For the first time that day I saw the judge smile, and returned it gratefully.

Hallelujah! I walked out of court a free woman into the happy, waiting arms of my family. Quickly I searched for my pills. The little yellow Percodans did the trick every time. I had to be careful about addiction. After taking the pills for any length of time, my body built a tolerance to them, making it necessary to take larger doses for the same relief.

Introduction to pills came with my first illness. What began as a slight pain in my lower abdomen, progressed to back pain and frequent urination, pain I could not push to the back of my mind. I soon went to the doctor, who diagnosed pelvic infection, a common ailment in women. He prescribed penicillin for the infection and Darvon for the pain. He promised relief from the infection within ten days. Taking the Darvon gave me the same feeling that drinking alcohol did, without the hangover. Instead of taking half a pill, I began to increase the dosage. Soon I was taking two at a time; I knew I needed to cut back. I had to stay off the pills for a period of time to break down the tolerance level, then I could begin again.

Darvon developed a craving for sweets. I often sent the children to the store for a supply of chocolate candy and soda. Food was second on my list. I could not believe what one little pill could do. I felt good. All my problems disappeared with a little red capsule. If being sick felt this good, I'd just grin and bear it. Soon the infection cleared up, but I continued taking Darvon.

When I thought I was healthy again, I returned to my former activities. Wherever I could manage to be seen, I was there. With time, bad diet, alcohol and promiscuity, the infections rapidly spread to other areas of my body. My GYN referred me to an urologist. He prescribed stronger medication, and bedrest. Keflex took the place of penicillin; Codeine #2 and #3 replaced Darvon.

Intentionally, I over medicated myself. I no longer waited for the weekend to get high. I got high at home on medications. As soon as my body was almost free of the infections, I returned to my habits, and the infections spread again. Finally, I required hospitalization.

I was given an IV the day I was admitted. My body had built such an immunity to the penicillin, Ampicillin, and Keflex, that they were ineffective against infection. The clear liquid flowing into my arm would now work against the infections. Codeine was replaced with Percodan during the day and Demerol injections at night. In my mental state, the high was what I wanted. The new painkillers were better highs than I had previously experienced.

I could stay high forever. Under their influence I could live a lie; I was in love; I had no problems. Food was unnecessary, therefore, I lost my appetite. The effects of the medication lasted about two or three hours, then I fell asleep. As soon as I awoke, my thoughts were on medication. After treatment, I was pronounced well and discharged, but my body never received total healing, due to my own neglect. I became even more dependent upon medications.

At home Darvon and Codeine were inadequate. I couldn't achieve the high I'd had in the hospital. When the doctor suggested Percodan, he wrote a prescription for 30 at one time. Sometimes I received prescriptions for 45 or 60. Although it was a controlled substance, I was able to get it whenever I desired.

I abused Percodan as I had the other legal narcotics. Taking one pill was too strong at first. By taking graduated amounts I soon worked up to three pills every four hours. Before long I was taking pills between the four-hour dosages. Realizing I was taking too much, I tried to quit.

74

I could quit for short periods, but needed a substitute for peace of mind. That substitute was one hundred proof alcohol. Drinking made the infection worse and increased the pain in my kidneys. I dropped the drinking and concentrated on the painkillers. When I was discouraged or depressed, I popped a pill.

As soon as I began to feel better physically, I began to try new drinks, new boyfriends, new clothes to fight the depression. The deeper I sank, the higher I wanted to be. I mixed drugs and alcohol for a bigger high.

Blackouts resulted. Many times I barely realized where I was. I found myself in places I did not choose. I searched my memory to remember what I had done the night before. I was ashamed, but blocked anything disagreeable from my mind.

My body and mind were too tired. My whole system broke down and I was hospitalized again. The infections took their toll. My insides were a mess. I was advised to abstain from alcohol, soda, spicy foods, and sexual intercourse. The doctors did their part; I did not do mine. When headaches began, and the medications I was already taking did nothing, I was prescribed Fiorinal.

One night in a bar, under the influence of alcohol, I developed a terrible headache. Just as I was about to pop some pills from the packet I carried, a hand shot out from nowhere. It knocked the pills from my hand onto the floor. Stunned, I looked for the person who had done it. I saw the young man at the same time I heard his voice.

"Are you crazy? If you take those pills with the amount of alcohol you have in your blood, you'll never live to tell anyone about it."

For a fleeting moment I was frightened. I intended to take the pills with my drink. I knew he was right, but I became angry. It was my life, and I could do with it as I desired. I left the pills where they were, only because pride did not allow me to be seen scrambling for them.

I was ready when an acquaintance asked me if I was interested in a blind date. I was not interested until he mentioned the guy had money. Once I met Wil, I immediately decided he was what I was looking for all along. I had the added pressure of two boyfriends, but after showing my closest girlfriend and neighbor the expensive gifts Wil gave me, she encouraged me.

After a late night with Wil, I came home to find Jay waiting for me. Then I found that my trusted girlfriend had told him of my activities. On my way to her apartment I tried to suppress the anger I felt rising. After a heated confrontation, she went to the hospital, and I went to jail.

Although grateful to be home from court, an uncomfortable feeling surrounded me. I felt doomsday was coming upon me. There was nothing I could do to stop it. No amount of pills or alcohol helped. Things were happening to my mind. I was going deeper and deeper into depression. Mentally unstable, I began to withdraw from everyone gradually. Had I withdrawn suddenly, someone would have noticed.

I covered my mood swings in various ways. First I withdrew from my children's friends. Then I got rid of Jay. He was too close.

The day he came to my apartment I could not speak to him. Something closed my mouth. I sat staring at him while he talked. Bad thoughts were racing, faster than I could think. I hated him. I hated all men. None of them could be trusted. They were only here to help themselves. Jay was responsible for my going to jail. I was the one left holding the bag. No more!

My thoughts exploded in a string of filth and "Get out! Get out of my house!" As he left, I said, "good riddance!"

I could see he was hurt, but I was beyond caring. I wanted to be alone with my thoughts, but the phone rang. It was my mother.

After I said hello, I could not speak. The same thing shut down my voice again. I could hear voices talking on the inside, but I could not speak. Mom wanted to know what was wrong. She did not hear the voices cursing her, but I heard them. I wanted to talk to Mom. I wanted to tell her that I loved her, but I couldn't. Something restrained me. It had more power than a voice. It did more than talk; it controlled my actions. If the voice said not to speak, I couldn't. If it said shut myself away, I did. He said I was depressed, and I was. I took my remedy for depression, even increased the dosage of pills, but the high was not high enough. I still felt sad.

The next morning I was barely able to get out of bed. I tried to make the bed, but the weight of it was too much. My normal duties were unbearable. I climbed back into bed, and then I remembered my children. They had to go to school.

I didn't know how I was going to manage. God bless the children. They understood mommy was sick and needed rest. They prepared themselves and went to school. Thinking I was alone, I was relieved, until I remembered the two little ones. They were hungry. I forced myself out of bed and gave them cold cereal. Turning on the cartoons, I instructed them not to move, I was sick and going back to bed. My children did as they were told.

Soon after that day I received a call from the school psychologist. She needed to talk to me about my son's school work. During our interview I began to tell the psychologist how I felt. She advised me that I was suffering from a depression that could be controlled by medication. As a psychologist, she could not prescribe medication, but recommended that I make an appointment with the mental health clinic immediately.

I pondered what she told me. I was not going to the mental health clinic. I was not crazy; I just had a few problems. In a few days I would be fine. If any of my friends knew I went to a "head shrink," I would be the laughing stock of the neighborhood. I quickly banished all thoughts of seeing a psychiatrist.

The same night I began experiencing other abnormal symptoms. Although I was absolutely tired when I went to bed, once I was in bed, I was instantly awake. I lay in the dark, listening for voices. I felt someone or something was in the room with me.

I dismissed the feeling and finally went to sleep, but every fifteen minutes something shook me awake. I felt tremors in my body. The next morning I struggled to climb from the bed. I was so tired and sleepy, I could barely function. After sending the older children to school, I wanted to cry, but couldn't. The house was a mess. Uncleanness had taken hold of me again. I rarely took a bath. Beneath the wig, my hair was matted on my head. I could not remember the last time I had combed it. When I ran my hands through it, it fell out in bunches. I found it easier to leave the wig on, for days at a time. I even slept in it. Now I hated my hair!

Going to my favorite place in the room, I realized too much light was streaming through the windows. Daylight meant exposure. I pulled all the shades and curtains and sat on the floor in the corner of my room to escape reality. Restraints were on me, which kept me rooted to the floor. Every second of misery became a reality. Loneliness closed in on me from all sides. I had friends, but no one could see or hear them but me. They instructed me. The room became my whole world, and I could not leave without my friends' permission.

I heard my babies banging on the door. They sounded like they were in the distance, yet the sound vibrated in my eardrums in echoes. I could not move until my friends let me go. When I felt released, I opened the door and tried to give the little ones breakfast. I dressed them and sent them outside to play. Leaving the dishes on the table, I returned to the place on the floor until it was nap time for the children.

That night I experienced the same patterns as the night before. This time the voices began to talk to me. They told me I was miserable. I had nothing to live for. I wasn't any good to my family in my condition. I could not provide for them. It made no sense to go on like this. I would be better off dead. Kill myself, they said.

They were right. They had just given me an answer. I was going to kill myself. As soon as I got the answer to my problem, I felt elated. Why didn't I think of that all along? It made sense to take my life. I wouldn't have to worry about anything. The comfort of those thoughts allowed me to sleep.

The next morning I did not forget. I awoke feeling better. I never had to be sad again. Problems in life were for the living. My problems would be over soon. I wouldn't have to worry about another day. I was going to find peace at last. The excitement of having a solution brought on a supernatural high that took me higher than pills. This was the ultimate happiness I had been seeking.

I felt I must move quickly, before someone stole it from me. The preparations were easy, because I was sure I was doing the right thing. I was even able to clean the apartment as I had in the past. Everything must be neatly arranged. I didn't want anyone to think I was a slob. I was perfect while I lived. It was required that people know I did the right thing. After all, I was a minister's daughter. My death will mean a lot. Everybody will notice that I am somebody. They will all cry and wonder how they could have helped me. No one had helped; I was alone.

I dressed the children and made sure everything was in its proper place. No sense in anyone having to do extra work on my behalf. There will be time enough for that after I am gone. Completing my chores, I sent the babies out to play. I was so proud of them. They were good little children. Soon they will forget all about their mommy. Someone will be there who can give them what mommy can not.

I sat on the edge of the bed to collect my thoughts. I needed directions on how to go about this. The time for suicide had arrived.

IX

SUICIDE

Like a person taking direct orders, I slowly left the bed and walked to the window. Opening it wide, I positioned myself at the ledge. *Soon it will be over. I have nothing to fear, because I am not alone.*

I thought of all the people I was joining as I looked beyond the grave. *There are plenty of people from all walks of life who can not cope with depression. It will be a peaceful place of rest where I can be happy. Those who are looking for a way out can find peace at last.* Just as I was ready to make my move, the sound of other voices penetrated my stupor.

"Mommy! Mommy! Come down and play with us." I heard the voices of my own babies. Little did they know how I was about to come down. I was intending to take my life. Immediately, I went inside to find the number of the mental health clinic. I suddenly realized I desperately needed help. The receptionist put a psychiatrist on the phone. She wanted to know if I was able to leave my apartment, and then instructed me to come in as soon as possible.

My "soon as possible" was the next afternoon. I did my best to get dressed. Beneath my wig my hair was beyond help, so I simply changed wigs. I could not leave the house without first applying makeup. As bad as I felt,

I still could not allow anyone to see me without makeup on my face.

On the way I rehearsed what I was going to tell the doctor when he asked me what was wrong. It seemed very important that I say the right thing.

The mental health clinic looked like any other building. I walked in slowly fearing I would break if I moved any faster. As I heard my name called, I noticed the psychiatrist coming toward me. He escorted me into the room where my psychiatric evaluation was to take place. After giving the doctor all the biographical information, we discussed the reason I was there.

The psychiatrist assured me, although he would ask many questions, I did not need to be afraid or embarrassed.

"Mental illness," he said, "is a sickness like any other illness. Try to think of it as an illness that can be controlled with medication."

He asked me to tell him in my own words what brought me to him. As I began to describe my feelings as openly as possible, multiple thoughts kept interrupting me. I heard them cursing in my mind. They tried embarrassing me by calling me stupid and lazy. They called me crazy, and they made me feel inferior. It slowed my speech and everything began to crowd in on me. I felt more depressed than ever. Of all times to cry, this certainly was not it. I didn't want to, but I could not control the tears. Strange voices began to laugh from within. I was a real mental case, and the psychiatrist knew it.

I described, what the psychiatrist called symptoms, as best as possible. After I finished he categorized them all together. His diagnosis was that I was mentally depressed with suicidal tendencies; although I had not successfully committed suicide, the tendency to do so was there. Mental depression was a symptom of suicide. The majority of people who considered suicide were depressed before that decision. My lack of appetite and its accompanying weight loss, was also a symptom of depression. Some patients experience excessive eating habits, followed by obesity. My case was the opposite, but he could not tell me why. He explained that my loss of sexual desire, loss of libido, was unnatural for a young, attractive woman. I should have an active, healthy sex life. Withdrawal and loneliness were also common symptoms. Depression caused me to withdraw from society, family members and friends. People who suffer from depression experience abnormal desires to shut themselves away.

When he asked me if I heard voices or had contrary thoughts, I began to answer, but thought better of it. If I told him I heard voices, he would know I was a basket case. I lied and told him I did not.

"Good," he said. "Things are not as bad as I thought. Many patients hear voices telling them to do abnormal things. Some claim it is the devil or the voice of God."

As the psychiatrist continued to describe depression, he mentioned that insomnia, sleeplessness, was common. I felt I had told him too much already; I had all the symptoms he described. I decided to tell him no more.

"Does anyone else in your family suffer from mental illness?"

I told him about my older sister who was diagnosed as mentally ill. She was committed to a mental institution a few times.

This information seemed to be decisive for the doctor's diagnosis. He concluded that I had a chemical imbalance in the brain, possibly hereditary, which caused the depression. I could have been born with the imbalance, or it could have been caused by an injury. There did not exist a medication to reverse the damage, but it could be controlled by medication. The field of psychiatry, he explained, is not an exact science, but great strides are being made every day.

Medication will successfully control my symptoms, and I will be able to function as a normal human being, **as long as I take the medicine.** I began to cry all over again. I did not want my life controlled by psychiatry. It invaded my privacy. This man told me I would be mentally ill for my entire life unless for unknown reasons I went into remission. Remission was not understood; he did not know if it would happen or how long it would last if it did. The symptoms could appear or just as easily disappear, but I should not count on that.

At the end of the evaluation, the doctor prescribed the anti-depressant Elavil, in 25 milligram pills. I had to stop all other narcotics, legal or illegal. Mixing Elavil with any alcohol was lethal.

He continued to explain the complex procedure and results of taking this drug. The dosage was one pill the first and second days, two pills the third day. After the third day I must return to have my progress monitored. After reaching the level of 75 milligrams, or three pills, I would maintain that level by taking one pill three times a day or all three at night. Most patients take them at night because Elavil acts like a sedative. The side effects would be a marked change in appetite, dryness in the mouth and throat, and extreme tiredness. All the side effects would fade as my body became accustomed to the drug, but the drug would not begin to take effect until a week or ten days.

Everything sounded so complicated. My mind did not comprehend how I was even in such a state. I was still hoping all this would just go away. The doctor's voice broke into my confusion.

"Some of our patients have been taking this drug for years. You may take it for a while and then begin to feel better. Your body could go into a remission period and not need the drug, or you may have to take it for the remainder of your life. I must caution you again about abruptly stopping the medication. You must gradually decrease the dosage the same way you increased it, one pill at a time, with our constant supervision. Stopping suddenly will give you more problems than you have now. Do you have any questions?"

I shook my head and began to cry again.

"I will see you in three days, Antoinette. The receptionist will give you the next appointment."

I asked for appointments after one o'clock, because I could not get up earlier than that. I left the doctor's office wondering how I had come to require psychiatric care. I never thought this could happen to me. I was not mentally deranged, but I was mentally ill. Medication was now my only ray of hope. The prescription in my hand determined my entire life.

I wondered what "chemical imbalance of the brain" actually meant. The psychiatrist said it was a malfunction in the brain. My brain did not properly produce the right chemicals, which caused depression. I did not understand all the terminology used to describe my problem. All I wanted was to understand what was wrong with me, and how I developed this. He said I could have been born with it.

Hereditary could explain my sister's history of mental illness; but why didn't my whole family suffer with it? My father had a strong mind. Mom was all right too. My brothers' and sisters' minds were fine. Why some of us and not all? Maybe mine was not hereditary. The psychiatrist said it could have been caused by an injury. The only injury I remember was a blow to the head at the age of eight. I was expected to lose the sight in my left eye. An inch difference in either direction would have killed me, but I wasn't even left with a scar. Could this have caused me to suffer depression?

As the questions rolled through my head, I wished the psychiatrist had more answers instead of creating more questions. My only hope now was in the little pills, and this time I followed his instructions. I did not drink or take any other medication. I did not want an accidental overdose. Suicide was no longer an option for me.

When I filled the prescription, the druggist informed me my Medicaid card did not allow payment for the medication; it was my responsibility.

By the time I reached my home, the tiredness the psychiatrist mentioned hung over me like a cloak. Although I was only in my mid twenties, I felt twice my age. I gave the children their dinner, but having no appetite myself, I skipped the meal. Maybe tomorrow I would have an appetite again. Why did some people overeat when depressed? He seemed to have no answers to my many questions. He said psychiatry was not an exact science. Suppose he was wrong about my medication? I didn't want to die. Anxious thoughts crowded me, and panic began to envelope me. If I lost belief in this medication, what would be left? I had to believe it worked.

At exactly 7 p.m. I took the Elavil. At 9 p.m. I was still awake, although all the children were sleeping. The last time I looked at the clock was ten; the next time, it was 7 a.m. I could not believe it! Where did the night go? I slept a drugged sleep. I had no sensation of being sleepy, however, the doctor's caution about being tired was an understatement. I was drugged stupid, but had to get the children ready for school the next morning. The dead weight made quick movements difficult. My mouth felt like the saliva glands had dried up. Water only helped for the time it was in my mouth. All day I felt as if my insides were lined with cotton. The doctor was correct about my appetite returning, but I was too drugged to cook and eat. I managed to prepare the children for school, fed the little ones, and set them in front of the T.V. surrounded by toys. I could do nothing more than go back to bed and sleep. Every time the medication lessened, it was time to take it again. I remained in the stupor for three days, until the time of the next appointment. The night before the visit, I increased the dosage to 50 milligrams as the doctor had said. I would not have kept the appointment if it had been earlier than 2 p.m.

During the second session, the psychiatrist did most of the talking. I was physically present, but mentally I only vaguely knew where I was. My brain felt numb. Although my thoughts were drugged into silence, I had no desire to commit suicide. I had no desire to do anything, certainly not talk to a psychiatrist. Speaking each word required great effort.

I told him my appetite had improved, but I was too tired to cook and eat. He could look at me and see I what I described. Sleep was more than a desire; it was a must!

He admitted that he expected me to be this way, and it was going to get worse before it got better. That night the dosage was increased to 75 milligrams, three pills at once. The drugged feeling, and dry throat and mouth would continue until my body adjusted to the medication. He also informed me that he was leaving, but a female psychiatrist would continue my care.

I looked at the doctor as if he was speaking a foreign language. I could barely function enough to climb from the bed with 50 milligrams of Elavil. He was increasing it to 75 milligrams. I requested that he call in the prescription for me, but he refused.

"Antoinette, I understand and sympathize with the way you feel, but I do not think it would be wise to do that. You've admitted to thoughts of suicide in the past. The medication you are taking is extremely potent. I would hate to see anything happen to you. If you find that you can not come in, we will send someone to your apartment for you."

His answer made me rampant with hatred for him and the situation I was in. Voices in my head were talking faster than I could think.

Me and my big mouth! Why did I have to tell him about suicide? I'm so stupid! I hate this place. I hate it... Thoughts carried me so far out, I did not realize the doctor was calling my name.

"Antoinette, are you listening to me? Did you leave for a moment?" I had.

"Yes, I understand what you are saying. May I go home now? I'm still tired and sleepy."

"You may go, but remember to get and keep your next appointment." I left the clinic feeling no better than when I walked in.

Night after night, I took the medication as I was instructed, and in the same state of depression, I went to sleep each night. However, approximately ten days later, it was all over. I awoke happy and excited! The world was a beautiful place; the medication worked!

As abruptly as the depression had come, it left, just as the psychiatrist had said. I was fine. Not only was the depression gone, but also the withdrawal, loneliness, suicide and despondency. Loss of appetite and sexual desire were gone; I felt like a woman again. I regained my pride and desired to improve my appearance. It had been a long time since I had felt this good.

The psychiatrist was right! All I had to do was be patient and the pills worked. Elavil became my wonder drug. With it I could do all things. As long as I was on the medication, I felt no depression. I had so much enthusiasm I cleaned everything in sight. Then I realized that Uncleanness was gone. I was pleased with psychiatry. It had the answer after all. So what if it came in a pill? I was normal at last. I could smile! I could sing and dance! **As long as I took my medicine, I was fine!**

Dressing with extreme care for my next appointment, I was eager to meet the new psychiatrist, because the old Toni was herself again. I walked in smiling. All my problems were solved.

My new psychiatrist came into the waiting room to introduce herself. I had no trouble relating to her. In fact, I couldn't quit talking. I just had to let this doctor know that they all were the greatest. All the contempt had disappeared. I did not mind seeing her, if it kept my sanity.

"Antoinette, I realize you feel okay now, but I want to caution you about the medication. You must continue taking the Elavil. Many patients make a common mistake. Once they begin to feel better, they become negligent about taking their medicine, and all the old problems, the negative behavior patterns, the thoughts and voices begin all over again."

"As long as you are on this medication, you must remain under psychiatric care. It is extremely important that we monitor your progress. Should the time come, we can increase your dosage to 100 milligrams a day. You will know when this need arises, because you will begin to feel as if the body is regressing back into the same pattern of depression. The former symptoms will reappear. It only means that the medication is not strong enough to ward off the depressed state of mind. This is not cause to panic. The body builds up a tolerance for the drug. You let us know if that happens, and we will increase the dosage. As long as you follow our advice you will be fine."

I felt that good things were going to happen to me now. I was going to live my life to the fullest. On the way home, I stopped by the department store to purchase a new wig. I left with a new wig and a job as wig stylist and manager. I now had a good excuse to ignore my own hair. The best way to sell wigs was to wear them. I demonstrated every wig in the store. I was a blonde, brunette, and redhead all in one week.

Elavil worked well in my system. My mind was clear; my body was clean; and I took pride in everything I did. I was able to work with no signs of laziness and had no side effects or abnormal behavior patterns.

The only problem I had was dangling two boyfriends at once. Pressured to make a choice, I chose money, which meant I kept Wil and got rid of Jay.

From the beginning, Wil showered me with gifts. He took me to fancy clubs and seedy bars. We frequented 42nd Street with its long string of theaters. All kinds of pornography was offered for viewing, including oral sex and masturbation. The actors were adept and influential. At the conclusion of one movie, we had a first rate education in filth.

When I returned home, the scenes lingered in my mind, and then began to play over and over. My body desired what I saw and my mind did not object.

Soon I was sick again, but Will was not as patient as Jay had been. He did not understand that depression is an illness. If he loved me, I reasoned, he would accept me sick, but I did not convince him. Knowing I was an embarrassment to him, I began to drink to cope with his attitudes. I made sure I was flying when he was due home. Although I was aware that alcohol had an adverse effect on my physical condition, I had to drink to calm my nerves. I could not understand how I let Wil do this to me. I thought I loved him, but there were times I could not even stand the sight of him. Any other guy I would have thrown out by then, but even when he mistreated me, I was quick to respond to him when he called. I did not like what I had become, but I could not control my obsession with this man or end our relationship myself.

The day he packed and left town, I felt like I had been freed from a two-year jail term. Immediately I agreed to take Jay back, and we picked up where we had been. At least Jay had compassion on me when I was sick, and he understood I had a need to see the psychiatrist.

Gradually the old patterns of laziness began to manifest itself. I lost the pride and satisfaction of work. My desire to work was slowly replaced with panic. I had to be free of my job. It was eight hours of confinement, five days a week. Day after day I dragged myself to work on my own schedule. I put a closed sign up for lunch and did not return for hours. My boss did not check on me, so he did not know why the business was declining. Rather than lose more money, he closed the business. My lack of desire to work, combined with the mental and physical problems, kept me totally dependent on Welfare. Either I received a budget deficit (partial assistance for working clients), or I received full assistance. Most often it was full assistance.

Now I felt relief knowing I was not required to get up and report to a job. I was free to spend my time doing as I pleased, and I was content to watch soap operas for hours. I became totally absorbed in their world of fantasy. Many days went by that I did not begin my house cleaning until the last soap opera was over. I could not seem to do without them. The leading characters on *One Life to Live, The Young and the Restless,* and *Days of Our Lives,* became my best friends. I drank when they had problems, and I drank when I had problems. I blended into their world of alcohol, tranquilizers, girlfriends, boyfriends, separations, divorces, adulteries, and murders.

My physical and mental condition began to worsen. I was not taking care of my body. The heavy medication, alcohol, and poor diet brought me to the point of self-destruction. The infection reoccurred, and I had to be hospitalized again.

When I was admitted, the Elavil was placed in the hospital safe until my discharge. I was not allowed to have it in my possession because I was on other medication.

Almost immediately my body began to feel the effects of the withdrawal. The first symptom was loss of appetite. Without Elavil I could not eat. The thought of food made me sick. The sound of the food trays being delivered to the rooms made me want to cry. I would rather have the pain than eat. The nurses tried to force me without success, until they threatened to feed me intravenously. Quickly I found another solution. I wrapped my food in paper and placed it in my roommate's wastebasket. No one bothered to check.

As the desire for sleep overwhelmed me, I began to sleep around the clock. The craving for medication took over the few waking moments I did have. Medication, combined with sleep, helped me escape reality. My doctor suspected I was sleeping unnaturally, because I was recovering from the infection well enough to walk around and shower on my own. However. when I tried to do so, I began to hemorrhage while in the shower. I was given no other hope but to let nature take its course. If nature moved in the wrong direction, my days were numbered. All I could do was stay in bed and wait it out.

My mental condition continued to deteriorate. I regressed into the more serious state of depression the psychiatrist had described. Gradually the withdrawal from Elavil began: mental depression, loss of appetite and weight, weakness, tiredness, sleeplessness, loneliness, withdrawal, uncontrollable desire for medication, lack of will to live.

As the thoughts of suicide began again, I knew I had to take Elavil again or I would take my life. Knowing the Elavil was unavailable, I asked for huge amounts of pain medication. The mental pain bothered me more than the physical pain. I cursed the day I left my Elavil with the hospital staff. No longer caring if I over medicated myself, I just wanted to die; but looking around the room, I found nothing. I was being closely watched, so I begged God to let me die.

In His mercy, He did not answer as I desired, but sent someone in the room to pray for me. Thank God for all the ministers and missionaries with hospital ministries. It was the prayer of faith which enabled me to leave the hospital room alive.

"Antoinette, your insides are a mess. You are a mighty lucky young lady to be alive." With those words the doctor allowed me to check out. I picked up the Elavil; my psychiatrist was right, I could not do without it, not even for a day. Without Elavil I was like a junkie without drugs.

I returned home weighing 98 pounds, knowing I was unable to cope with my family. I had to see my psychiatrist. In ten days my system adjusted to the medication again. I saw the immediate results of increased appetite and began to gain weight. No longer desiring to commit suicide, my outlook improved to the point that I forgot how sick I had been. I returned to doing my own thing.

No sooner had I started living life to the fullest than I was hospitalized again. I had a terrible headache, which stretched all the way down my back. The accompanying dizziness and nausea caused my equilibrium to malfunction. My medical doctor instructed me to see her immediately.

She discovered my blood pressure was much too high, so she put me on a salt-free diet. That was the hardest for me. From childhood I had eaten salt without even tasting my food. I had had many warnings about excessive salt, but I could not control my usage of it. After ten days in the hospital, I was released to battle the high blood pressure.

I did not adhere to the diet, but I did keep my appointments with the psychiatrist. We talked about everything that came to my mind, but one day I began to think the sessions were useless. I began to feel I could do without psychiatry. Not wanting the withdrawal I had experienced in the hospital, I finally voiced my thoughts to my psychiatrist. Seeing that I was adamant about it, she agreed to let me try to withdraw gradually under her care.

After a few days I felt fine. This stretched into weeks, and I knew my hunch was right. I had overcome mental depression. My body had gone into remission! No more Elavil! No more psychiatry!

The psychiatrist could not say how long it would last, but I knew with a miracle, it could last forever. I felt so good I found a job doing what I enjoyed most, other than styling wigs. I began work in a day care center as a teacher's aide. I loved my work and everything in my life seemed to be normal.

The only other major change of events was that Wil returned to town. All he had to do was call, and we were back where we started. As the old lustful desires came rushing back, I forgot all about Jay, who had nursed me back to health. I forgot his compassion and our calm relationship. I traded it all for a stormy relationship with Wil. Soon I was sneaking around to see Wil and trying to hang onto Jay. Finally I just chose Wil.

My mother could not understand me. She tried to talk me out of seeing Wil again. My family and friends could not understand why I knowingly chose such a destructive life, so I began to close myself off from anyone who criticized Wil. I was not ecstatic with him, but for some reason I was hooked on him and could not let go. Although Wil had not changed, I had one thing on my side this time. I would not be an embarrassment to him because I was seeing a shrink. Those days were in the past.

As hard as I tried, I still could not live up to Wil's standards, and I became a nervous wreck trying. While Jay and I were together, I had put my life together again. Now everything seemed to be going in reverse. As soon as Wil came around me, my body began to tense. I had never suffered from nervous problems before, yet I shook like a leaf when he was near me. I thought one day this man was going to cause me to breakdown, yet I still could not let go of him. My nerves became so bad, I took an indefinite leave of absence from the day care center. The indefinite leave became definite. Nervous tension prevented me from working with the children.

For almost a year I had been fine without medication. I refused to believe all my old behavior patterns were returning. Not wanting Wil to know that I was slipping into a depressed state again, I began to drink to cover up my depression and physical weakness. When he was around, the alcohol gave me enough boldness to put on a show. I knew my acting was not enough, but I refused to return to the mental health clinic. Instead I went to the medical doctor for my nerves. I just wanted something to quiet me. He gave me a prescription for Valium every four hours.

I took Valium as often as possible. The 5 milligrams did calm me for a while, but soon I was taking 10 and 15 milligrams. I switched from Valium to Tranzene, to Librium, back to Valium. Those tranquilizers were good for calming me down, but I also needed something to pep me up, so I tried them with alcohol. When that was not enough, I tried Darvon, Codeine, Percodan, and Fiorinal for the headaches. Nothing was completely successful; I was being carried further under, increasingly more depressed. Even when suicidal thoughts began reoccurring, I refused to seek help. I was willing to try anything but psychiatry.

I lost my desire to work anywhere. The very thought of work repulsed me. Why should I work; I was receiving a welfare check. At the first of the month, I joined the crowd waiting for the mailman. After he arrived, we joined long lines to cash the checks. The money never lasted longer than a week, but so what; it was good while it lasted. There was always another month to follow. During the month without money, we managed somehow. We all had boyfriends.

When the law was passed that required mothers on public assistance with school-aged children to work or go to school, I panicked. I hated the thought of being employed, or being made employable. I did not want to go to school and work was out of the question. I dodged every appointment the Westchester County Agencies arranged for me, but authorities in the Work Incentive Program, run by the County of Westchester, did not give up easily. Due to the overcrowded system, they were not able to keep accurate records of my whereabouts, and I was able to slip through the system. However, after a run around that lasted well over a year, the agency labeled me as unreliable and irresponsible, and I finally appeared for an appointment. I sat in the office and lied; I gave every excuse I could generate for not keeping my appointments. Because I had a history of illness, I managed to keep my welfare check coming. I was allowed to remain home supported by welfare and caged by Wil.

I felt like a helpless animal backed into a corner. Wil was my master, and whatever he said was the way it was. I had one escape: pills and alcohol. At night I took downers to sleep. During the day I took uppers to make me high. Still I had to come down and face reality. When I did, my mind could not handle the load.

Thoughts of suicide began to torment me worse than ever. When an image of the window ledge loomed, I was forced to go to my psychiatrist. I did not want to die. Unless I received help, I knew I would take my life. The day I returned to my psychiatrist, all my pride and dignity had been stripped away. I was less than a woman, finally ready to accept anything psychiatry had to offer.

Contrary thoughts and voices had a good time making me feel incompetent. *Who am I to think I can beat mental depression and suicide? I am a nobody who tried and failed. Many people greater than I had been brought down thinking the same thing. The graveyards are full of them. I should be grateful that in the face of the strength of mental depression I am still alive.*

When my psychiatrist asked me what I had been doing since I had last seen her, I gave her partial answers. I told her all the good things, such as my former job, social life, the work with underprivileged children.

When she asked about my present activity, I had to admit, I wasn't doing very much. She thought my present depression was caused by inactivity. As long as I had been active, she said, I was fine. Now, to be inactive, could have brought on the depression again.

As she continued to inquire about me, she asked if I had a boyfriend. At the mention of "boyfriend" I began to withdraw. I thought it best to keep Wil a secret. Everyone must believe that I was happy. I had made mistakes before; I could not fail now. Perfection did not allow for mistakes. Pride did not allow me to speak of errors.

The more the psychiatrist talked, the deeper I withdrew. My own thoughts closed me into a world of silence. I withdrew so deeply from reality that I could only hear the thoughts and voices from within. When the voices spoke to me, no one was allowed to intervene, but the doctor was unaware of what was happening in my mind. All she could see and understand was my outward manifestations. I could not speak, and she had no knowledge of why. The voices had much to say to me, but they did say anything aloud. They only talked to me.

I understood my personalities, their behavior patterns and desires. The first personality in control was a female who hated men, and she talked to me without being intimidated by the presence of the psychiatrist. Had the doctor been a man, I would have been angry and lost control, because no man could tell me what to do. Men had ruined my entire life.

All my personalities were agreeing with psychiatry, especially this woman psychiatrist. She was in complete control, No one could tell her anything. She was dominant and forceful, just like I should be.

I was thinking so fast, I lost my awareness of time. I began to be disoriented and confused. I was remembering, but not far enough back. On the verge of an answer, I forgot. Frustration set in, and I wanted to cry, but I could not. Instead an image of my boyfriend appeared before me, and anger and hatred for him took control of me. *I hate Will and what he is doing to me. He is not my boyfriend. He is a man destroying me. I have to get rid of him in a hurry before he gets rid of me. I am a woman in control! No man tells me what to do. Men only hurt. They use you and throw you away. I have to pay this man back for the way he is treating me.*

Multiple thoughts, voices and personalities joined together. I felt a surge of power go through me. *I can do anything! I am not afraid of anyone! Enlightenment! I can finally see clearly now. I can remember now, thanks to the voices. They inform me who this man is and what he has come to do. He is not the kind, gentle person he appeared to be in the beginning. He is my enemy. He is the one destroying my will to live. He knew I could not stand silence or rejection, but he rejected me by not speaking to me for days. He forced me back into the world of silence I had been closed in before. The loneliness was unbearable. Because he disliked my family and was jealous of my friends, I closed them off. He was all I had.*

Each thought made me more angry. *I know I have never been as faithful to any man as I have with Wil, but that was not enough for him. When Wil began to go out at night, and I heard him return at four in the morning, it reminded me of my first marriage with Tim. So I had to pay Wil back, and I did with a couple of one-night stands. Revenge motivated me to do it, and it was bigger and bolder that I was. I had every right to do as he did. After all, I am a woman, aren't I? All women have to stand their ground. I never regret. I proved I could do what any man can do, maybe better. It doesn't matter; I hate him. I hate them all! I will destroy myself before I let any man take advantage of me!*

If he had not lied about having money, I would have some consolation. But he lied about that too. He had no money! Not only was he a liar, he was a thief. He has left me with nothing, not even my self-respect.

I am at rock bottom now. This man stole my womanhood from me. I have no desire for sex. No libido, and no one to report it to, because he had not broken any law. No sense to voice this to the psychiatrist. Her only answer is medication. I have to take matters into my own hands. No man must ever steal from me again.

One of us must go. He will kill me if given the chance, but I must never give him the chance. I am a survivor, but I need help. Help will come soon. It is in the palm of my hand. When I get ready, it will be over quickly. I hate men, and one day soon, I will finally get my revenge. After that day I want nothing to do with any man. Psychiatry can not stop me. She has no knowledge of how to get rid of me. Her only answer is medication, but medication does not determine my destiny. I always follow my thoughts.

Once the voices ceased, and my thoughts slowed down, the confusion and disorientation left. I was able to hear precisely what my psychiatrist was saying. She knew nothing of the encounter I had just had, but the voices were right about one thing. The only hope psychiatry offered was medication. She immediately increased the Elavil from 75 to 100 milligrams a day and said if problems arose to let her know.

Before long I began to feel the uneasiness of depression. Anxiety returned, bringing with it a fear of going to prison that I could not explain. Paranoia about men took all desire for male companionship. My appetite dwindled to almost nothing. I began to understand what the psychiatrist meant about needing more Elavil. I needed more just to function. The doctor increased the dosage to 125 milligrams a day; only then was I able to retain my sanity.

As a result, I regained pride in my appearance. The lazy feeling subsided. My appetite returned, and I began to gain weight. Although sexual desire returned, I wanted nothing to do with Wil or any man. I needed love, but I had given up hope of ever experiencing love from a man.

About this time, my brother-in-law opened his own business. He asked me to manage the selling end of it. With much persuasion, Wil agreed to let me. During my time at the store I had closer contact with my sister. She was one of the first of many blessings which turned my life around. She witnessed to me about the word of God that she heard in a church she was attending, the Bible Church of Christ on 100 West 2nd Street in Mount Vernon, New York. She told me about the love she had experienced there, and that I should give it a chance.

I had been in many churches, and I was tired of being the object of the preachers' sermons. I had never been in a church where the love flowed as my sister described. I thought everybody was on the take, and I was tired of being taken, so I had no interest in going to church. I did not believe there was a church anywhere that could make me feel better about the ministry. Rather than poison my sister's mind, I just quietly declined.

When depression returned with anxiety, nervousness, crying spells, withdrawal, and hatred of men, my medication was increased to 150 milligrams a day and no promise of ever decreasing it. I had tried to withdraw from

Elavil, but failed. I had believed in remission, but it proved to be a lie. I was now worse than I had been when I first saw a psychiatrist. My present dosage was double that first one. I knew that I could only function as a normal human being as long as I took the medication. When Elavil proved ineffective, there would be another medication to take its place. As the medical doctor said in the hospital, "Let nature take its course."

My sister did not succeed in getting me to church, but God did. I was not aware of it then, but God used the man from whom we purchased supplies for the store to witness to me. He was also a minister in the Bible Church of Christ. After his effective witnessing, I agreed to give church a chance.

The very day I stepped into the Bible Church of Christ I found that my sister was telling the truth. Love was the foundation of the ministry. The love of God was manifested everywhere. Love touched my stony heart and melted it down to flesh. The hardness of my heart began to disappear under the spoken word of God. The negative attitude I had about all ministries was replaced with a positive one. In the very first visit I was a changed young lady. Little did I know that it would be within this ministry that God would draw me by His Spirit, and a work would be done in my life beyond human understanding.

PART II

FREE AT LAST!

X

DELIVERANCE

"Well, Nettie, how did you like it?" my sister asked.

"I loved it!" I was so full of joy, I could hardly contain myself. Something had happened to me in the Bible Church of Christ. I did not know what it was, but I did know I wanted it to happen again. From the moment I walked into the church, I could feel love drawing me. No one looked at me as an outsider. If God could bless me by simply saying so, then I was indeed blessed by many just saying "God bless you."

I came into the church expecting to be put down because of many bad experiences I had in other churches. There were times in the past that I had attended church to satisfy a longing to be there, but once I was there, the preacher's sermon was directed at me. My clothes were attacked. My appearance was criticized. Once I was even pointed out as the young lady who had come with earrings in her ears. I was so embarrassed that I pulled them out. Hurting inside, I resolved to never go back. No preacher was going to tell me how to dress or what to do. The Bible Church of Christ had high hurdles to jump to win my soul.

Instead, the entire service, from Sunday School at ten in the morning to the end of the morning service at noon, was a special blessing. I was fine until the bishop stood up to preach. I immediately began to tense, waiting for him to say something about me. I had vowed in my heart I would

105

get up and walk out if that happened. To my surprise, I heard nothing of the condemnation I expected. He preached the word of God, unadulterated, without bias, the first I had heard since hearing my father preach. As I relaxed, I felt the tension leaving. My body, soul, and spirit were soothed. At the same time I became aware that I was a sinner in need of salvation.

I understood for the first time John 3:16. "For God so loved the world, He gave His only begotten Son, that whosoever believeth in Him should not perish, but have everlasting life." I was part of the world this man mentioned in his text. Although I was a sinner, Jesus Christ loved me enough to die for me before I was born. God was a forgiving God no matter who I was and what I had done. The sermon was love. The message was lengthy, but when it was complete, I had been convinced by its powerful ministry.

After the sermon there was more. The pastor and preacher, Bishop Bryant, Sr., offered a prayer line for those with needs. He explained to first time attenders that we would probably see things we had never seen, but not to think it strange, or to be afraid. It was the power of God.

I had seen and heard prayer in church before, so this did not frighten me; but I had not seen a prayer line, and I was not ready to get into it. Much to my amazement, I saw people get in line and by the power of God, were slain in the Spirit. One lady was in line on crutches, barely able to walk. When Bishop Bryant prayed for her healing, she began to run around the church praising God. Her crutches were left behind.

Some were in line to receive the baptism of the Holy Ghost. I saw Bishop Bryant lay hands on their heads and/or bellies and say, "Receive ye the Holy Ghost in the name of Jesus." The individuals began to thank Jesus in English and their language changed right in the middle of it. I heard different languages come forth while the congregation praised God.

About 3 p.m. the service ended. To my surprise I had spent the majority of the day in church; I had never spent a better day in my life. I had come with nothing, but I left overflowing with the love of God. It was enough to stabilize me until I could get back to the Bible Church of Christ the next Sunday.

Four weeks later, on a Sunday in February 1980, I knew I wanted to receive the gift of the Holy Ghost. I had a terrible struggle getting to church that morning. At two in the afternoon I was still trying. At 2:30 I was walking into the church just in time to hear Bishop Bryant say, "It is prayer time in the Bible Church of Christ." He called for two lines, one for healing, and deliverance, and the other for those who wanted to receive the gift of the Holy Ghost. I stepped into the second line with three other women.

In the name of Jesus, Bishop Bryant gently placed his hand on my forehead. The first thought in my mind was faith. This man certainly had an incredible amount of faith. He knew I would receive the Holy Ghost. With authority he said, "In the name of Jesus, receive ye the Holy Ghost!" The power of God went through my body. Beginning to thank Jesus for His gift, I ended up on the floor, speaking in tongues just as the word of God records in Acts, Chapter 2.

Hallelujah! I walked into that church at 2:30 and received the Holy Ghost before 3 o'clock, along with three other people. I found it did not take God long to do anything. I had been raised in the Apostolic (Jesus Only) Doctrine, which taught that seekers have to "tarry" to receive the Holy Ghost according to Luke 24:49: "And behold, I send the promise of my Father upon you; but tarry ye in the city of Jerusalem, until ye be endued with power from on high."

I thought it took time to receive, that we were to tarry

until we came through. I had been in tarrying services. Some tarried for hours, others for weeks and years. Some never came through. I had called on the name of Jesus for hours until I was weary and just gave up trying. No one in my former church understood that the Holy Ghost was already here and all we have to do is receive Him. No one exercised the gift of laying on of hands. I had been taught misconceptions, because the word of God was not rightly divided. Scriptures were taken out of context, which generated confusion. One scripture said it all, and the other scriptures were cause for arguments. The full gospel taught in the Bible Church of Christ proved what I had been taught to be half truths. That day's experience was just the beginning of my understanding of the full gospel.

"Rightly dividing the word of truth" meant to take the total Bible, not just parts to fit what we have conceived in our own minds. Jesus did command his disciples to tarry, or wait, in the city of Jerusalem until the Holy Ghost came. The 120 believers, including Mary, the mother of Jesus, were waiting in the upper room when Pentecost came, according to Acts 1:12. Fifty days after Passover, and ten days after Jesus' ascension, the Holy Ghost came just as Jesus promised. Because the Holy Ghost has already been sent, on that day of Pentecost, we no longer have to wait. Through the laying on of hands, which was practiced by the disciples, the apostles, and Jesus Himself, people in any day can receive the baptism of the Holy Ghost.

The first thing I did after getting off the floor was go into the lady's room to wash my face. The makeup on my face suddenly felt heavy. I wanted my face to be clean. Afterwards I returned to my seat, and my six year old son asked me, "Mommy, what happened to you down there?" I told him I had received the Holy Ghost.

"Is that why your face is shining, Mom?"

"I guess so, Nate."

My son was right. My face had a glow that no cosmetics could give; it came from within. The best thing was no one in the church had pointed to me as the young lady with the heavy makeup. Nor did they single out my apparel. The people let the Holy Ghost take charge of whatever needed to done within me or without.

I was a willing vessel. Hearing the full gospel made me realize that Jesus Christ had a massive cleaning job in me. Bursting with excitement, the first person I told was my mother, the moment I returned home. Then I ran next door to tell my neighbor what had happened to me. The change was so pronounced that no one could deny that a miraculous experience had occurred in my life, not even Wil.

That same Sunday evening he walked into the house and just stared at me. Joy from the Holy Ghost made me smile. I could not contain it.

"You got the Holy Ghost today, didn't you?" I asked him how he knew.

"I can see it all over you. Even the house feels different."

He began to tell me that he did not think he could live with that. He made no bones about it; he could not tolerate it. For the first time in years I felt peace. I did not care what he thought or how he felt, because I had a friend who "sticks closer than a brother." His name is Jesus Christ. I held my peace, began doing my normal chores, singing on the inside.

My mind felt so good that I leaned on Jesus more and more each passing day. The Holy Ghost gave me enough power to leave my house without first painting my face. He took away the pain of rejection by Wil. He gave me peace and took away the fear of dying.

These experiences that I now had with Christ, and the word I was being taught at church enabled me to make a major decision that proved the field of psychiatry wrong.

I decided to stop my medication, and instead, take on the mind of Christ Jesus, as written in Romans. That very day, I quit taking the 150 milligrams of Elavil I had been taking daily.

That same month, February 1980, announcements were made of a mass deliverance service to be held in the main sanctuary of the church. I began to hear testimonies about people delivered from spirits of witchcraft and suicide, snake spirits, and disco demons. Many professed to be healed; others received the Holy Ghost. Although the service was not to be held until March 3rd, I knew by the grace of God I would attend.

After a week without Elavil and no repercussions, I awoke with a slight disturbance in my mind. From past experiences I knew what it was. But in light of my recent experiences at the Bible Church of Christ, I was going to try Jesus in the prayer line.

Sunday afternoon, when Bishop Bryant called for the prayer line, I immediately joined it. I whispered to him that I wanted him to pray for my mind. He laid hands on my head and prayed for peace of mind. I immediately felt the soothing effect of the Holy Spirit. Mental depression subsided, and I did not have to take Elavil or return to the psychiatrist. God proved to me that "Thou wilt keep him in perfect peace, whose mind is stayed on thee: because he trusteth in thee. Trust ye in the Lord forever." (Isaiah 26:3,4.) Through prayer I received total peace of mind. When I put my faith in the Word of God, He honored it.

Saturday, March 3, 1980, 8 p.m. at the Bible Church of Christ is a night that is etched in my memory forever. Almost three weeks after I received the baptism of the Holy Ghost, I entered the mass deliverance service as a skeptic. I did not know what to expect or what to do regarding "deliverance." The sanctuary was crowded; at least 500 people were there. I looked around to see if I could spot any demons. I had heard that the demons were inside people, and they would be cast out during the service. I wondered if any of these people had demons. They all looked normal to me.

That night the church held an element of reverence that created expectation and joy among the people. The anointing of the Holy Ghost was so great that it vibrated like electricity in the entire church. Praising the Lord was as natural as breathing. One couldn't help but praise the true and living God, who was in our midst to bless His people. After the praise, prayer, and singing, our pastor stood to teach, aglow with the Holy Ghost anointing.

He explained that the teaching would be necessarily long, but through it demons would be exposed. We were all handed paper that held a drawing of two hands and some paper towels. The paper held a diagram from *Pigs in the Parlor,* a book written by Frank and Ida Mae Hammond. Each finger was a different spirit, including schizophrenia, depression, and suicide. They included spirits of psychiatry called phobias, fears, abnormal behavior patterns, and personalities. Bishop Bryant call them demons, and I believed him. During the teaching I made up my mind that I would get rid of mental depression that night. I was not totally sure of the procedure, but followed what everyone else was doing. When the teaching was concluded, Bishop Bryant announced he would pray the deliverance prayer.

We all stood and lifted our hands to Jesus. Not only did we pray, but under Bishop Bryant's leading, we renounced the spirits by name, saying aloud that we no longer wanted them in our bodies. This disallowed their claims on us. I did as I was told.

With determination, I loudly said, "Mental depression, I don't want you anymore! I hate you! I want you out of my body and my mind! My mind belongs to Jesus!" And I meant every word.

Still, I did not know what to expect. I simply followed instructions, because I had never seen a

111

deliverance service, but being obedient to the instructions paid off for me in this service. After the prayer we all took our seats. Bishop Bryant had already explained how he would call them out by the spoken word after we had renounced them. They would have to leave under the authority of Jesus Christ.

Jesus called out many demons in His ministry. Some He allowed to speak, while others He commanded to hold their peace. A man of God carries the same authority today. The Bible states in Mark 16:17,18 "And these signs shall follow them that believe; In my name shall they cast out devils; they shall speak with new tongues; they shall take up serpents; and if they drink any deadly thing, it shall not hurt them; they shall lay hands on the sick, and they shall recover."

As Bishop Bryant began to call out innumerable spirits, I stayed in a prayerful mood, but I could not help but watch what was happening around me. No one was talking or laughing, but demons began to cry out of people in loud voices. Some people covered their ears in order not to hear. They heard anyway.

In the name of Jesus, demons were being cast out and people were rejoicing in their freedom. When Bishop Bryant called mental depression, I felt a pull in my body the same time I heard a moan from my mouth. I thought it was just me, and I desired to remain quiet, not disturbing the service. But the moan became louder, and I clapped my hands over my mouth. My body began to rock back and forth. I had no control over what was happening to me. Soon Bishop Bryant went on to other spirits and my feelings and movements ceased.

No sooner had I sat back to relax than he called out mental depression again by name. He began to talk about the mind and commanded depression to loose the minds of God's people. The feeling in my mind could withstand the commands no longer. I saw my behavior patterns change immediately as I let loose a high-pitched wail. I knew the wails were not me, but those of the demon of depression. I was trying not to disturb the service. Over and over again I screamed. My body began to rock at an incredible speed; my head started shaking. Although the demon of depression was being tormented, I had a peace that even mental depression could not disturb. I understood the scripture in John 14:27: "Peace I leave with you, my peace I give unto you; not as the world giveth, give I unto you. Let not your heart be troubled, neither let it be afraid." Down deep inside, I felt no fear. The perfect love of God had cast out all fear. I wanted this demon out at all cost.

Soon one of the workers in the deliverance service came over to me. She told me to release the mucus in my throat. Softly, she began to speak the Word of God in my ear. I was thinking that I had been on a fast for three days, therefore I had nothing to cough up. But that did not matter. I coughed and a blob of mucus came forth into the paper towels provided for us. At that very moment something happened. The torment was gone. The depressed state of mind left, and it was replaced with a feeling of peace and comfort. I was free at last! I felt I could say with honesty that I was finally clothed in my right mind.

Immediately I began to praise God and cry. It was all over. After my praises, I began to smile. It was a smile of joy that engulfed my entire being. The years of torment due to mental depression were finally over. Jesus did not let me down. The ministry I received in the deliverance service proved psychiatry to be a lie. I could not help but remember that the doctors had said that depression was hereditary, a chemical imbalance of the brain, that I would have depression the remainder of my life, and take Elavil, even increase the dosages. But in Philippians 2:5 God's word states "Let this mind be in you, which was also in Christ Jesus." Jesus Christ's mind is not depressed.

After that unforgettable Saturday in 1980, I have had no need to take any type of anti-depressants. I have not heard from mental depression. Deliverance is stronger than medication and it lasts longer than remission. It hits the problem at the source rather than dealing with symptoms. I had two things on my side from that time forth. I had been baptized with the Holy Ghost, and I had a free and clear mind. Through Christ I could now do all things. I could even withstand what was going on in my home. My home became the second area the Holy Ghost was transforming.

God was still moving on my behalf. Wil continued to witness a remarkable change in my life, which he did not like. He gave me an ultimatum: either the church or him. I chose the church. Still not believing I would go that far, he gave me an extension of one week. He moved into the living room until I came to my right mind on the matter, but I never gave in. Little did he know I had previously lost my mind; now it was replaced with the mind of Christ. A few weeks later he moved out of my home and out of my life. God set me free!

"Wherefore come out from among them, and be ye separate, saith the Lord, and touch not the unclean thing; and I will receive you, and will be a Father unto you, and ye shall be my sons and daughters, saith the Lord Almighty." II Corinthians 6:17,18. God himself separated me. I had to do nothing but live holy.

I continued to walk in the love and grace of Jesus Christ. Although I was growing spiritually, physically I was losing more weight. I thought it was normal weight loss until people in the church began to notice. While we were enjoying one of our fellowship dinners, Bishop Bryant remarked that I ate barely enough to keep a bird alive.

Later on Bishop Bryant questioned me about my weight. He was quite concerned that I was so much smaller than my sisters. I explained to him what I thought the problem was.

"This is normal for me. I do not have much of an appetite, and I was never able to gain much weight. When I first came into the church, I weighed 143 pounds, only because I was taking Elavil, which is an anti-depressant and appetite booster. It allowed me to have a healthy appetite. When God delivered me from mental depression, I no longer needed the Elavil, so my appetite and weight have dwindled. To tell the truth, I eat very little, next to nothing."

Bishop Bryant told me that was not normal; that one day he was going to pray for my appetite.

I pondered what he said, and began to be concerned. I had lost about 40 pounds and was still losing. Finally I went to my medical doctor. The nurses, who had not seen me for a while, were alarmed because I had lost so much weight. They and my doctor were in agreement that it was not a healthy loss. The doctor prescribed a liquid appetite booster to take daily. I tried it, but it made me so sick I could not keep it on my stomach.

Loss of appetite was a stronghold in me as I continued to lose weight. This became evident at an anniversary dinner for our pastor. I intended to work in the kitchen until I began to inhale the aroma of the food and became sick. I actually hated the thought of trying to digest any food. I went home without eating a bite, realizing something was seriously wrong with me. I had not eaten a full meal for some time and still had no desire to eat. The next time I saw Bishop Bryant, he voiced concern again about my appearance. I had lost 43 pounds.

On a Friday night the church held a deliverance service at the The Bible Church Of Christ (Headquarters) at 1358 Morris Avenue in the Bronx. When Bishop Bryant began to teach, I realized the Holy Spirit was speaking to me through him. His topic was maintaining correct eating habits. I listened intently until he began to talk about an undereating demon. Strange things began to happen to me. Someone was trying to block what I was hearing, someone inside of me. Suddenly I let out an uncontrollable giggle. I couldn't help myself. Trying not to disrupt the service, I put my hands over my mouth from time to time to hide my strange actions and sounds. Soon the giggling stopped, but it was replaced by contrary thoughts.

That's a lie! That man is lying! There is no such thing as an undereating demon. People overeat, but people don't undereat! I could feel myself ridicule everything Bishop Bryant taught. I could not understand why I suddenly felt so contrary. I tried my best to ignore the contrary thoughts, and soon they ceased altogether.

After the teaching and the group ministry, Bishop Bryant held a prayer line for those who felt they needed individual deliverance, or those who needed more deliverance. I suddenly remembered that Bishop Bryant had said he would pray for my appetite. And I desired to eat!

Suddenly anxious thoughts began to encourage me to sit down. I felt I'd be a fool to get prayer for an appetite. My thoughts called Bishop Bryant a liar. They said they hated him; the closer I came to Bishop Bryant at the head of the line, the more anxious my thoughts became, and the more foolish I felt. They became so persuasive that I finally sat down.

But thank God for the Holy Ghost. I John 4:4 says "Ye are of God, little children, and have overcome them: because greater is he that is in you, than he that is in the world." The power of the Holy Ghost was greater than these thoughts. He lifted up a standard from within, and I rejoined the prayer line.

When I stood up again the anxious thoughts became angry ones. They began to threaten my life. They said they were going to kill me because I wouldn't shut up. I was called every filthy name there is. The closer I came to Bishop Bryant, the more I desired to run, but I remembered the teaching that same night. "If we feel like running in these sessions, don't give in. It could be that a demon wants us out of the church in order to escape exposure."

The teaching helped me battle the temptation to run until I reached the head of the line. Still unaware that I needed more deliverance, I merely reminded Bishop Bryant that he had promised to pray for my appetite.

Smiling at me, he said, "That's not hard at all, Sister." He gently laid his hand on my belly and began to pray for an appetite. Instantly the top half of my body began to turn completely around. My mouth opened wide, and the same abnormal thoughts I heard earlier became an angry voice that spoke aloud.

"Shut up! I told her to shut up. We are going to kill her." The voice was angry because I prayed. It was angry because I came to Christ, because I had lost the spirit of mental depression. For about ten minutes Bishop Bryant worked with me to cast the spirit of undereating out of my body.

Finally, the demon could stand the anointing no longer. He hollered, "You can have her; she's yours!" I spat out mucus and was free.

No one had to tell me to praise God for my deliverance. It was spontaneous and joyful. Marvelous are His works. After losing the second demon in my life, I realized my loss of appetite was the activity of a demon called undereating, which worked with the demon called mental depression. It was not a symptom of depression as psychiatry stated. He was a demon with the intent to kill.

In a matter of weeks I gained twenty-six pounds. The weight gain strengthen me, and added to the peace and joy in my heart, contributed to a Holy Ghost glow that no medication can give.

The deliverance I experienced not only set me free of demonic spirits, but it also taught me that the thoughts I was having and the voices I was hearing were not my own. Abnormal behaviors and perverse sexual desires belonged to different demons, each with their own distinct personalities. Each demon did according to his name. Mental depression worked in the mind to cause depression. Thoughts of depression may not have been my own. Undereating did not allow me to maintain healthy eating habits. His job was to close off the appetite. His direct purpose, as with all demons, was to kill and destroy.

Psychiatry labels undereating and anorexia as mental problems. Deliverance proved to me that these were also demons working with the demons of depression and suicide. Psychiatry will not understand this because "the natural man receives not the things of the spirit of God: for they are foolishness unto him: neither can he know them, because they are spiritually discerned." I Corinthians 2:14.

What psychiatry considers foolishness has saved many minds. I have been free since 1980 and am still going strong in the grace of Jesus Christ without medication or psychiatry. The Holy Ghost is my keeper. For "I know in whom I have believed, and am persuaded that he is able to keep that which I have committed unto him against that day." II Timothy 1:12. I have committed my mind to Jesus Christ!

However, God did not stop there. On Wednesday night during our weekly prayer service I received a miraculous healing for an "issue of blood." I was finally healed of the pelvic and kidney infections through the laying on of hands by our ministers. I obeyed the command in James 5:14. "Is any sick among you? Let him call for the elders of the church, and let them pray over him anointing him with oil in the name of the Lord."

My doctors had given up, so I knew if I were ever to be well, it would come through the ministry of the church.

The ministers gathered together, and the Elder laid hands on me and prayed for divine healing. The power of God went through me like fire. When I realized what had happened, the pain was gone. It happened instantly. "And the prayer of faith shall save the sick, and the Lord shall raise him up; and if he have committed sins, they shall be forgiven him." James 5:15.

I have had no reoccurrences of the infections since that day. Jesus Christ became my Healer as well as my Savior. "But he was wounded for our transgression, he was bruised for our iniquities: the chastisement of our peace was upon him: and with his stripes we are healed," Isaiah 53:5.

XI

DEMONS SPEAKING # 1

"Please, Bishop Bryant, help me! I awoke this morning at two a.m. with tremors going through my body and voices calling my name. The voices were inside me. They know who I am, and they know all about you. They say they want to speak to you. One is a female named Jezebel. She sounds like the old me! I can hear her saying the same things I used to say before I received the Holy Ghost."

I was almost hysterical on the inside, but trying to remain calm on the outside so Bishop Bryant could understand what I was trying to say on the telephone. I had waited until 10 a.m. to call him with what sounded so unbelievable.

The voices woke me saying, "Antoinette, are you awake? Hello, dear. My name is Jezebel.

"You've changed, Antoinette. You never used to let a man tell you what to do. No more, Antoinette! No man is going to tell me what to do! You've gotten stupid! I hate Roy Bryant! He is not going to tell me anything! Do you hear me, Antoinette? Stand up for yourself, after all, you are a woman!"

Before I could get over the initial shock of hearing the exact duplicate of the old me, another angry voice intervened. He used profanity that I had not used since receiving the Holy Ghost.

"I hate Roy Bryant! I hate his radio broadcast! It is to be stopped immediately! I want Roy Bryant stopped!. He had gone too far in this ministry."

With horror I listened as the voice told me in explicit detail how they and their master, Satan, would seal up the Bible Church of Christ with all the people inside and burn them alive if the preaching against the Roman Catholic doctrine across the airways did not stop. This voice wanted me to tell Bishop to back off the stand he had taken. He was to stop preaching that "Jesus Christ is the only mediator between God and man. My master, Satan, also known as the god of this world, has millions believing that the Pope is the mediator. The Pope is god to the Roman Catholics!"

Continuing to explain the incident to Bishop Bryant, I told him that I felt an additional intruder. Each time I felt this one move, I recalled my pastor's own deliverance from the spirit of pride. Although I kept trying to ignore these memories, they did not go away.

"There is still another spirit in me, Bishop. He hasn't identified himself, but I believe it is the spirit of Pride. I can feel him, but I can't hear him. It has to be Pride."

"Do you feel proud?" Bishop asked.

I tried to collect my thoughts in order to answer his question. Thinking back, I recalled the times God used me. After each incident, my chest puffed up. I felt like I had done something great. It was a feeling of "look at me. See who I am!" I knew this was not the Spirit of God, and I did not like the feeling. I tried praying and fasting also, but it did not leave.

"It does sound like Pride, Sister," Bishop Bryant confirmed.

Explaining the remainder of my early morning encounter, I told him that the tremors stopped when the voices quit. About six a.m. the phone sweet voice of Jezebel called me again by name.

"Good morning, Antoinette. Are you awake?" I heard her hideous laugh. I was sure I hated her.

When I had tried explaining these occurrences to the psychiatrist, he had given me medication. Someone had to believe me, and help me. The voices were real. They lived inside my body. They talked, moved, cursed, and destroyed. They were very real, although I could not see them. If it were possible, I would have clawed my way inside my body and pulled out these strange invaders.

Bishop Bryant's words were different than any advice I had been given. With complete assurance and comfort, he believed me and understood what I was experiencing. His recommendation was not medication, but deliverance. He described what was going on and who was in my body with me. They were disembodied, rebellious spirits, with personalities of their own. They were now manifesting themselves in my body in order to satisfy their own lusts.

The demon's message to Bishop Bryant did not alarm him. He had experienced Satan's tactics before this. I was comforted that he believed me; he did not think I was crazy. Just talking to someone brought immediate comfort, but Bishop Bryant promised to take action that would set me free.

He assured me that just as I had lost the demons of Mental Depression and Undereating, we would get rid of the spirits of Jezebel, Cursing and Pride. He asked me to come for deliverance to the headquarters on Friday night immediately after his radio broadcast. I couldn't help but smile at the irony of that. The demon would have to hear what they hated most, the radio broadcast. I knew Bishop Bryant would not compromise his message because of the threats I'd heard.

When I hung up the phone I felt a surge of power through my body. The force was so strong, it engulfed my entire being. I had no alternative but to ride with it. It was not me, but another personality, whose name was Corrupt

Communication. With profanity he cursed the radio broadcast, Bishop Bryant, and the Bible Church of Christ. As soon as he withdrew, the same surge of power happened again. Another personality came forth. Her name was Jezebel. She was a man-hater, and she made no bones about how much she hated Bishop Bryant. He was not going to tell her what to do. "After all," she said, "I am a woman and no man will get rid of me!"

When she completed her message I was able to straighten up for a second before I felt I had to be recognized for who I was. I was somebody! I was not just anybody! I was someone of importance. I was KING PRIDE!

Boasting, he said, "I want to meet Roy Bryant. *I* want to talk to him. *I* am the same one who was in Roy Bryant, and *I* am now back ten times stronger. He got rid of me one time, but he will not get rid of me again. *I* am going to use the gifts that God has given you. *I* am going to allow you to come up, and then *I* am going to bring you down!"

Once the surges of power subsided, I was myself again. After regaining my own identity I felt tired, frightened, and disgusted with Satan. What I experienced was more than a change in personalities. They were demons fighting to retain their control. Now that their future in me was in question, their desires were unmasked. Their mannerisms, speech, likes and dislikes were so close to human personality, I had not discerned their demonic natures.

Although I did not want to meet Pride, I was glad to know this puffed up feeling was not me. God does not use a spirit of Pride. "God resisteth the proud and giveth grace unto the humble," I Peter 5:5. Remembering my pastor's testimony of his own deliverance from the spirit of Pride, I realized he was going to have another encounter with that spirit.

When the demons stopped, I went into the bathroom to pray. I began to question why all this was happening to me. What did I do wrong? I'd tried my best to live holy. I wasn't a hypocrite. Why God? God reassured me through His word: "My people are destroyed for lack of knowledge." Hosea 4:6.

During my prayer I began to understand that I would soon be through this ordeal. I could trust Bishop Bryant, because he had much knowledge and experience dealing with demons. The demons talk out of me, but not to fear. I would be delivered. When Satan has a message, let him talk. Let these things be documented. Then people from all walks of life can see God's victory and come to the knowledge of the truth.

After the time of prayer I broke down and cried. The demons began to attack my mind again. I never knew a human body could go through so much at the hand of Satan. I knew for sure that the thoughts and voices I had heard for years were demons. The multiple personalities I'd experienced since childhood belonged to demons. With all I had learned, there was still a great deal more to come. For the next few days, until my scheduled deliverance, I was tormented and ridiculed. My awareness of the demons made it more difficult to carry three personalities that did not belong to me.

The demons became bold about who they were and what they wanted. They made no bones about the fact they wanted to destroy me. I slept very little at night. Once I was in a comfortable position, the demons jerked my body, and I was unable to resume sleeping. If I did manage to fall asleep, Jezebel called me by name. Then I heard her and the cursing demon.

Later in the week I had the courage to talk to the evil spirits. I wanted to know what they wanted. They told me they wanted to address Roy Bryant and the Bible Church of Christ. They wanted him to know he had gone too far with his deliverance ministry. He had disturbed their master, Satan, and he was in a rage. Never once did the demons used my pastor's title; they always addressed him by his first name. They told me I knew too much, I had seen too much. I had too much knowledge. Perplexed, I asked them what it was I knew. I was told to shut up, I'd find out soon enough.

When I could take no more, I went into the bathroom and turned on the shower so my children could not hear me break down and cry. I did not want to experience this. I did not desire to hear demons speak from me, and I did not want them to use my body to address the whole church. When I could withstand no more, the Holy Spirit raised a standard against the spirits, and I acquired a peace that surpassed all understanding.

Friday night finally came. I arrived at the headquarters location with the help of Mary Parker, one of the church's missionaries. Realizing I was in deep trouble, she took care of my every need. Once inside the church, I desired to take my place in the broadcast's choir. Although I could feel the activity of the demons, the Holy Spirit kept me under control. The music of the choir soothed my spirit, although it made the demons angry.

Satan's anger was aroused when Bishop Bryant arose to preach. I could feel the demons watching him out of my eyes with an intense hatred, which permeated my being. If I had not had the Holy Ghost, I would have leaped across the pews, into the pulpit, and gladly strangled him. Although I felt the hatred in me, it was not me, and the Holy Spirit was still in charge.

The message that night was the one Satan wanted stopped. Bishop Bryant introduced Jesus Christ as the Mediator to the world and the churches. "For there is one God, and one Mediator between God and men, the man Christ Jesus." I Timothy 2:5.

He also refuted the lie of purgatory. Revelation 22:11 states "He that is unjust, let him be unjust still: and he which is filthy, let him be filthy still: and he that is holy let him be holy still." In Hebrews 9:27 "as it is appointed unto men once to die, but after this the judgment." The sermon was concluded with Philippians 2:10,11. "That at the name of Jesus every knee should bow, of things in the heaven, and things in the earth, and things under the earth. And that every tongue should confess that Jesus Christ is Lord, to the glory of God the Father."

Those in the radio audience heard that Mary, the mother of Jesus, was just a vessel who God used to bring His Son into the world. Mary also had to receive the baptism of the Holy Ghost, with the evidence of speaking in tongues as the Spirit of God gave utterance. She was in the Upper Room with the 120 on the day of Pentecost, according to Acts 1:14.

The demons within me were in a state of torment. They were screaming inside me, yet I did not utter a sound. The radio broadcast was uninterrupted, and the demons were forced to hold their peace. I began to experience what the writer of Hebrews said in chapter 4:12: "For the word of God is quick, and powerful, and sharper than any two-edged sword, piercing even to the dividing asunder of soul and spirit, and of joints and marrow, and is a discerner of the thoughts and intents of the heart." The word was so sharp I could feel it dividing between me and the evil spirits. The Holy Spirit was better than a sedative as He kept me calm throughout the broadcast. Near the end I did have to put my hands over my ears. The demons could stand no more of the gospel and its power.

When I put my hands over my ears I had the urge to run from the church. Satan had plans for me to run into the path of a car. As quickly as those images flashed in my mind, I entertained thoughts that an oncoming car might not kill me. Other choices were offered to avoid the eminent deliverance. The forces within me knew they were facing danger, and they wanted me dead. I could feel my desires change as different attitudes and emotions emerged. The shift in personalities occurred as each demon desired to have its own way. One wanted to address Bishop Bryant, while another wanted me dead. Another did not want to talk to him, because he feared the powerful man of God.

Although I felt the urge to run, I could not! The Holy Ghost was greater than the demons within me. Announcing the deliverance service, Bishop Bryant called me to the front of the sanctuary. As I began to walk toward Bishop Bryant he took a few steps to meet me. Uncontrollably, I backed up although I was unafraid of him. He seemed to look past me and began to address the demons.

BISHOP BRYANT: I thought you said you wanted to talk to me. Why are you running?

CURSING DEMON: I didn't say I wanted to talk to you. It wasn't me. She's seen too much. We have more in here than me. This is your fault. God is not going to use her. She belongs to my master. She knows too much. She's coming back with us. You #@$%@! Jezebel is in here.

She's been raping the prophets. We are destroying the ministry. Toni's seen Pride. She's seen Jezebel. She's a dreamer, just like you, Roy. We're gonna bring her down. We tried to destroy your radio choir, and this #$%$@ joins the choir. We're not coming out of here.

Bishop Bryant began to pray and call out the demon in the name of Jesus. My emotions were completely engulfed by the demons wishes, but I knew the profanity coming from my mouth was not me, but the cursing demon. I heard words that night I had not been able to control until I received the Holy Ghost. My speech and behavior took on the personality of three unclean spirits. As Bishop Bryant continued to pray, the same demons that had tormented me all week began to whine, beg, and bargain with the men of God.

CURSING DEMON: We promised our master. We can't kill her. Please, Roy! Please!

BISHOP BRYANT: You are going to come out of her, and you're not going into anyone else in this building.

Very quickly and suddenly the cursing demon withdrew. Immediately I stopped cursing and took on an attitude of seduction as the spirit of Jezebel came forth.

JEZEBEL: I am going to spiritually rape her, Roy. You are not going to have her. Who do you think is taking the prophets? It takes a woman to do a man's job. I'm not going to destroy her, I'm going to help her. She interprets dreams. She's seen too much. We are going to take her. I am a woman, Roy! You can't tell me anything! I am not coming out of her! You are in for a bigger shock!

After Jezebel spoke, she immediately withdrew. Another spirit, proud and boastful, replaced the spirit of seduction as the demon of Pride emerged. The personalities shifted as each demon manifested. My voice, mannerisms, and desires changed when the demons changed. I realized multiple personalities were demonic spirits.

PRIDE: I am Mr. Pride! King Pride! You got rid of me once, but you will not get rid of me again! Her life or yours, Roy! Shut up that radio broadcast! Leave the Pope alone! Stop telling the people that Jesus Christ is the Mediator. It's the Pope! He's god to the Roman Catholics! He's God! The Antichrist is already here! Nothing you can do about it! The scriptures must be fulfilled!

BISHOP BRYANT: Come out of her, in the name of Jesus!

PRIDE: We are not coming out. No!

BISHOP BRYANT: Spirit of Seduction, Jezebel, come out of her. OUT of her in the name of Jesus. Loose her.

I could hear, see and feel everything going on around me. My first thoughts were of the message the demons were delivering to the church. It was true. They did have a message for God's people, and they were speaking the truth according to the word of God. The devil was serious business and not to be taken lightly. Yet the man of God carried the ultimate authority. As Bishop continued to pray, his language changed into the heavenly language as he prayed in the Spirit. The demons were weakened and broken up, and I began to cough. In English he again called out Jezebel. At the mention of her name, Pride withdrew and Jezebel emerged.

JEZEBEL: I still hear you, Roy, and I'm not coming out.

BISHOP BRYANT: We got rid of Undereating, and we are getting rid of you. The Blood of Jesus. Pray Church!

The power of prayer rang out as the saints began to pray in one accord.

JEZEBEL: My god is Satan. I have to obey my master. I can't come out of her. My master will destroy me. Please, Roy!

At this time the same demons who had bragged about their authority, began to whine and plead with the man of God. I felt my personality shift again as Jezebel withdrew and Pride manifested himself. This demon, who claimed to be so strong, begged to keep his home inside my body.

PRIDE: Don't make me humble. Please, Roy. Don't make me humble. No, Roy. I'll call you anything, Bishop Roy Bryant. Don't make me humble, not in front of all these people. Please, Roy, I'm finished. You're destroying me. Don't humble me, please. I can't take this.

The Spirit of God is Holy Ghost fire. The word says that our God is a consuming fire. With this anointing and the laying on of hands Bishop Bryant had the power to cast out the spirits. Pride, the spirit of exaltation, was forced to humble himself, and it destroyed him. Bishop Bryant told Pride to leave in the name of Jesus, and he did.

I coughed up mucus and was set free. Immediately I felt the release in my spirit. I enjoyed my freedom from

Pride until my personality changed, and Jezebel came forth. She claimed Pride was her brother and began to cry for him. Tears streamed down my face uncontrollably. Logically, I had no reason to cry over the loss of Pride; I was happy Pride was gone. Without a doubt, it was the demon, Jezebel, who was shedding the tears.

JEZEBEL: Pride is gone, you stupid fool. He's gone. He doesn't have a second chance. (crying) You destroyed my brother, Roy.

BISHOP BRYANT: I know where Satan's seat is. I call you out in the name of Jesus. Come out of her, Jezebel.

Jezebel was weakening. I could feel the anointing taking her strength. Bishop Bryant and the people helping him continued to pray and command her to loose my body.

JEZEBEL: I'm getting weak, Roy. Don't make me come out. God is going to use her. We can't have that. My master wants her back.

BISHOP BRYANT: Come out of her, and leave this building!

JEZEBEL: We are going to pay you back. Roy, let's make a deal. We can't let Jesus have her. She's seen too much. Please, Roy! She'll be clean. She's enough trouble. She's destroying our kingdom. She knows about the Jesus Only sect. We've got them separated and fighting about water baptism. Please, she's talking to the Jesus Only people. Please!

Bishop Bryant began to speak in tongues. Then he commanded Jezebel to leave. On her way out, she let loose a hideous scream. To be sure she was gone, Bishop double checked, but I was praising God. It was over. From age twelve I had suffered at the hands of Jezebel. From thirteen I had suffered from Pride. I had begun to curse at age nine, but when I was thirteen, it was a stronghold in me. The longest week and the worse years of my life ended in victory.

"Therefore, if any man be in Christ, he is a new creature. Old things are passed away, and behold, all things become new." This had to be what the word of God meant. No one had the power to make me a new creature, within and without, but Jesus Christ.

The spirit of Jezebel, who told me that I was ugly unless I painted myself, was gone. The Bible recorded that Jezebel painted her face and tiered her head. This was the same Jezebel who took authority from her husband and destroyed the prophets of God. She is still destroying men today. She committed murder over and over. She is treacherous, deadly. The same Jezebel played a big part in my marriage and helped in all my adulterous affairs. She schemed, cut men down, and used me to do it. The world exalts and embraces woman's liberation, yet there is no known freedom like the freedom of Christ Jesus. When a woman rebels against the authority of God, watch out. Jezebel is waiting.

The puffed up feeling of pride was also gone. I was free of the many times I had walked the street, knowing I looked good to the world, and no one better tell me otherwise. My mirror told me so. My cosmetics said so, and above all, Pride said so. Even after I received the baptism of the Holy Ghost, Pride tried to play a part in the spiritual gifts God gave me. In Daniel 4:37, Nebuchadnezzar's words are my guide. "Now I, Nebuchadnezzar, praise and extol and honor the King of heaven, all whose works are truth, and his ways judgment: and those that walk in pride he is able to abase."

XII

DELIVERANCE BY TELEPHONE

"Sister, Toni, hold on real tight and get into a comfortable position. I am going to cast this demon out of you over the telephone." As Bishop Bryant spoke, I felt my body tighten and the familiar change in personalities. The spirit of Religion was fighting to control me. He began to address Bishop Bryant on the phone as he manifested himself.

"I know who you are, Roy Bryant! My name is Religion! I have Toni and I am going to destroy her. You are too far away. You can't help her now."

Although the demon of religion was boasting of his intentions, I could feel the soothing effect of the Holy Spirit as Bishop Bryant began to pray. The combination of prayer and anointing was so powerful that Religion threatened to hang up the phone.

"You don't have the power to do to destroy her," Bishop Bryant informed him, and he was correct. I never released the phone. The Holy Ghost within me was greater, and He kept me rooted in my position.

With the voice of a man, Religion continued to speak threats using my body to do so. He was so angry I watched my right hand pound the table uncontrollably. For ten minutes we were in spiritual warfare, but I had no doubts about the outcome. Bishop Bryant prayed using the name of Jesus until I coughed, and Religion screamed as he left my body. Joy engulfed me; "If the Son therefore shall make you free, ye shall be free indeed," John 8:36. After praising God in tongues I remembered to thank Bishop Bryant before hanging up the telephone.

I had called Bishop Bryant for help that morning because Religion had awakened me and thrown me off my bed. Then he cornered me on the floor in the position of a wild animal. My head was thrown back, and I heard false tongues coming out of my mouth. I knew they were false because of the teaching I had received at church about Satan's attempts to counterfeit the gifts of the Holy Spirit. I knew the tongues were not the peaceful tongues of worship.

Catching a glimpse of myself in the mirror, I was terrified to see the distortion of my face. The demon stretched the skin so taunt the veins protruded on my neck and arms. He gave a message in his false tongues and then interpreted it in English.

"I know who you are. I know Roy Bryant. The same God that sent him, sent you. I know what both of you have come to do. You will not succeed, because *I* am going to use the gifts God has given you. From now on *I will prophesy! I will teach! I will speak!* Do not call Bishop Bryant because he cannot help you. He is in the Bronx, and you are in Yonkers. You are too far away. You are finished, Toni!"

After speaking, the demon withdrew. Totally frightened, and a little confused, I made my way to the phone. I knew I had to do exactly as the demon instructed me not to do, but as I reached for the phone, Religion manifested again. He grabbed my throat and temporarily cut off my air. He made it plain I should obey him.

Letting go of my throat, he said, "I know what you are going to do. Do not call that man!" I inched my way back to the phone. Religion began to back down.

"That man, Roy Bryant, has too much power," and he began to whine, fearful that Bishop Bryant would get rid of him. That was all I needed to hear. As soon as Religion withdrew, I called my pastor and explained what was happening.

My resulting deliverance proved that distance is no barrier to the power of Jesus. I also realized that the demons' wisdom is very limited. They must recognize the extent of Jesus' power.

I John 4:1 states, "Beloved, believe not every spirit, but try the spirits whether they are of God; because many false prophets are gone out into the world." All voices, all guidance, all spirits must be tried by the written word of God. Not everything or everyone we hear is the voice of God. Since my deliverance, I have had no urgency to speak and be heard in church. God is not a blabber mouth. Now when I speak, I have peace that Satan's demons are not using my speech, although I still test the message by the word of God.

Christians should guard what they hear. Demons can enter through the ears and then build strongholds in other parts of the body. Even the telephone is an abused communication. We can now Dial-an-Anything by phone and hear pornography from the inspiration of perverse sexual spirits. Many of our children's sexual educations are occurring on Dial-a-Porn. May God have mercy on the ones responsible for filling souls with filth by way of the telephone. Some say "we are what we eat," but we are also what we hear and accept.

XIII

SELF-DELIVERANCE

"You are stupid, Antoinette! You were always stupid! Stupid! Stupid! Stupid!"

Before my own eyes I saw my features change. I looked like the old me, ugly. No one had to tell me that the demon of Stupidity had surfaced. Once he called me names and manifested his presence, I felt my muscles relax and my face return to its normal appearance. I was in control again.

I left the bathroom mirror and went into the bedroom to lie down, but a second area of attack began. Sexual fantasies began to play on my mind. Lust went from my mind to my body. Thinking I could sleep if Lust was satisfied, I masturbated. Afterwards I felt ashamed, used, and dirty, but I knew if the need arose again, I'd give in to it. I needed help. Lustful desires were becoming uncontrollable, but who will help with such a closet sin, especially in someone who has the Holy Spirit?

I planned to keep masturbation a secret. If I could get rid of Lust and Stupidity, I'd have no need to masturbate, and the unclean feelings would disappear.

When I was totally disgusted with what was happening, I spoke to my pastor about the abnormal sexual desires. Without surprise or condemnation, Bishop Bryant explained the differences of lustful spirits. Some are specific, others general. They often inhabit several areas of the body, including the sexual organs, but also the eyes. It is important to pray about all the types of demons.

Handing me a tape he had made on self-deliverance, he suggested I study it and try self-deliverance. If I was not able to dislodge the spirit of Lust on my own, he would pray for me. He had created the tape because the demand for deliverance had become greater than his capacity to minister. Wanting God's people free motivated him to use every means possible to reach more people.

Little did I suspect the mighty power I held in that cassette. He mentioned two to three hundred names of spirits on the tape, and gave the same instructions he gives in deliverance services. Following his taped instructions set me free; the Holy Spirit's power was just as effective as in a deliverance service.

Bishop Bryant cautioned on the tape not to play with deliverance, but to choose the baptism of the Holy Ghost as a follow up to deliverance, if the person has not already received. In Matthew 12:43-45 is written

"When the unclean spirit is gone out of a man,
he walketh through dry places, seeking rest,
and findeth none. Then he (evil spirit) saith,
'I will return unto my house from whence I came
out;' and when he is come, he findeth it empty,
swept, and garnished. Then goeth he, and taketh
with himself seven other spirits more wicked than
himself, and they enter in and dwell there: and
the last state of that man is worse than the first.
Even so shall it be also unto this wicked
generation."

I took the tape home that Tuesday evening. Since I was not working, I had the opportunity to use it the following day. Following instructions, I made myself comfortable on the floor and placed my Bible beside me and the stereo within reach in order to control the tape easily.

I was tired of being stupid. I was tired of masturbating, and tired of sexual lust taking advantage of my body. I desired to live holy, but unless I lost the spirits, I would be hindered. I wanted to present my body as a living sacrifice, holy and acceptable unto God, as Romans 12:1 describes.

As I heard Bishop Bryant's voice on the tape calling out the spirits, I immediately reacted. What happened next was beyond my expectations. He called out a demon of medication and immediately my body tensed. I opened my mouth and the words "She's eating Anacins!" came from it. "It's not my fault; she's eating Anacins!"

The demon was telling the truth. I had been suffering from terrible headaches, and I was taking many Anacins three to four times a day. I had long since ignored the recommended dosage in the instructions. My dependency upon medication was so strong I took pills when I awoke to prevent headaches that might occur. Just before bed I took more to prevent awaking with a headache.

This medication demon told on himself. He liked to eat medicine. In the past he enjoyed Percodan, Darvon, Librium, Valium, Demerol, and Darvoncette. Now that I no longer required those strong medications, he was satisfying his lust with anything he could convince me I needed, which was massive doses of Anacin. God delivered me from medication, and the reasons for taking it. His name was Headaches. Once I lost the demon of Medication, I also lost the demon of Headache.

As the tape played on, Bishop Bryant called out the spirit of Laziness. I heard a voice, not my own.

"Her mother said it! Her mother said she was a lazy girl! It's not my fault. She's lazy! She's lazy!"

I listened to the demon accuse me. He had discouraged me working for years, often successfully. Now

139

the Holy Spirit delivered me as I was obedient to the instructions on the tape.

Today, I am employed at a full time job. My day begins at six a.m. and ends about midnight. I work on the job, at home, and in the ministry of Jesus Christ.

Bishop Bryant called out the Hair Falling Out demon. My hands flew to my head, my fingers wrapped around my hair, and the demons cried, "Who told this man we are in here? Where did he get his knowledge? Nobody knew we are in here!"

The knowledge came from the Holy Ghost. Hair Falling Out was cast from my scalp. As a result I no longer have to wear a wig to cover my hair. I love my hair. It is soft, manageable, and continues to grow.

Bishop Bryant began to attack the spirit of Poverty. That demon was sure I would always be on welfare. He told me I was poor, but Poverty lied. The only thing poor is Poverty himself.

After losing that demon I have been able to support my household without the benefit of assistance. When I run short, I stand on God's word: "But my God shall supply all your need according to his riches in glory by Christ Jesus." Philippians 4:19. He keeps me spiritually, mentally and physically rich.

He has taught me also that paying tithes is very important in order that my finances are not cursed. In Malachi 3:8 is written,

> "Will a man rob God? Yet ye have robbed
> me. But ye say, wherein have we robbed
> thee? In tithes and offerings. Ye are cursed
> with a curse: for ye have robbed me, even
> this whole nation. Bring ye all the tithes
> into the storehouse, that there may be meat
> in mine house and prove me now herewith,
> saith the Lord of Hosts, if I will not open
> you the windows of heaven, and   pour you

out a blessing, that there shall not be room enough to receive it. And I will rebuke the devourer for your sakes, and he shall not destroy the fruits of your ground."

Now I find it a special blessing to be part of a ministry where I can freely give my tithes and know it is being used for the glory of God.

The demon of Anger surfaced.

"Don't call me by name, Bishop. If you don't say my name I won't have to come out."

When Bishop Bryant identified the demon by name, he lost his claim to my body. Since losing that demon, anger does not rise in my body like a heat wave, causing me to sin. I know now that anger is a human emotion that God has given to show our displeasure at things that are wrong or unjust. But He has also written "Be ye angry, and sin not: let not the sun go down on your wrath: neither give place to the devil." Ephesians 4:26,27.

I heard another voice, that of a salt demon. Salt said, "There is no such thing as a Salt demon."

Although he tried to remain unidentified, he could not. Knowing he was exposed, he changed his tactics.

"It's her fault. She always ate too much salt. She let me in here." Demons can tell the truth, when they feel it gives them the advantage or they want to boast. Salt was correct; I did use too much, but he lost his home during that deliverance.

The demon of High Blood Pressure followed Salt. I no longer take medication for high blood pressure and enjoy eating all my food without salt.

When the name, Stupidity, was finally called, I was immediately delivered. The last demon I lost during this session of deliverance was Hinderance from Reading God's Word. Amazed that these demons were so common and glad that they were mentioned on the tape, I coughed one

141

more time. The demon left my body with no trouble. I felt praise as I've never felt before.

"Behold the Lamb of God which taketh away the sins of the world." John 1:29. I knew He had cleansed me of my sins and taken the source of more. I saw instant relief. I no longer eat or crave medications. The desire for pills disappeared completely, and I am no longer plagued with abnormal headaches.

After losing the demon of Stupidity, I graduated from business school with an A average. I was the young lady who hadn't been able to succeed at anything, and had been exempted from the psychology exam. James wrote "If any man lack, let him ask of God." Knowledge comes from God. During my two-year course of business school I learned to depend only upon the Holy Ghost. He brought me through in all circumstances. I am no longer faced with poverty. I thank God for a country that takes care of its own by supplementing the needy with welfare. It was a blessing for me and needed at the time. Now, however, I work a full time job, with no signs of laziness, and am the sole support of my family. The rent is paid, food is on the table, and clothes are on our backs.

I am gratified that I am no longer hindered from reading God's word. One scripture that is especially meaningful to me is Psalm 1:1.

"Blessed is the man that walketh not in the counsel of the ungodly, nor standeth in the way of sinners, nor sitteth in the seat of the scornful. But his delight is in the law of the Lord; and in his law doth he meditate day and night."

XIV

DEMONS SPEAKING # 2

I want to be the apple in the top of the tree, Daddy. This man has dragged me all the way down to the bottom. I hate him! I hate him! Look what he's doing to me, Daddy. Please don't let him. Please help me, Daddy. Where are you? I've got to wash; I can't tell Daddy I'm dirty. But it won't come off; I can't get clean.

I am not your little girl any more, Daddy. Don't let them get me. They're evil and they're dark. They're nasty! They want to take me out of the church, but I want to write. I am still going to write for Jesus. I can hear the words in my mind. They are in my head. I gave Jesus my heart. I don't want to do these things. Their nastiness is creeping up my body. Stop these things from using me. Please don't punish me, Daddy. It not me; she's having sex. Don't punish me, I can't help it. Please, Daddy!

I was in the middle of another deliverance session at our Mount Vernon church. I arrived with the help of our missionary, Sister Mary Parker. The service began as usual with singing and praise, but the demons took control of my body movements and began to speak through me before the singing ended. They were stirred up and angry.

They said Bishop Bryant must pay for taking away a prize possession. Profanity came forth first, then verbal abuse and threats.

"Get your hands off me! She won't do nothing! She won't obey! It's your fault, Roy Bryant! She's ours! You have stepped on the wrong territory this time! You have really made a mistake! I am going to scandalize your name! You won't be able to hold your head up in this place!"

Quickly the demon withdrew himself. In horror I watched myself go from one age to another. My personality changed so swiftly, I lost track of who was speaking within me. Painful memories surfaced verbally.

"I'm going to have a baby. I'm too young. Daddy talk to me. It's her fault. She said I was ugly. She told me to paint myself. She said I would be clean. She dresses me up. Please believe me, Daddy."

I heard Bishop Bryant addressing the demons that spoke from my childhood. When he called Childhood Rape by name, the demon became extremely angry, knowing he was identified. From the anger emerged Hatred for Men. I grabbed the man nearest me, Bishop Bryant, and began to fight.

"I hate you! I hate you! I was a clean little girl, and you took everything I had. I am going to pay you back if it's the last thing I do," I said.

Although Bishop Bryant was not the guilty party, the demons twisted my perceptions. All I saw or understood was that any and all men should pay for the abuse. Using the discernment of the Holy Spirit, Bishop Bryant listened to the demons and my pleas for help and determined the number and names of the demons involved. He identified Self-devaluation, Self-destruction, Self-Rejection, Suicide, and Hatred of Men. The spirits were none too happy about being named. Hatred of Men spoke.

"You are going to need a miracle to get us out of her."

Bishop Bryant let him know he had a miracle, and his name was Jesus. When he began to speak in tongues, the demon withdrew and Corrupt Communication emerged.

"Give up the deliverance ministry! Too many people are hearing. Let it go. She won't work for my master. He said to destroy her. She is now going to talk my language. You're in enough trouble with my master. The radio isn't enough. Now it's television. How far do you think you are going with this ministry, Roy Bryant?"

Placing his hands on me in the name of Jesus, Bishop Bryant said, "Our God is a consuming fire."

Holy Ghost fire and anointing caused the demons to cry out, "You are destroying the psychiatry business. They are ours. People come in here and listen to these testimonies. Because of you and this deliverance ministry, they are watching and believing. They are beginning to believe there is hope for the mind. You are coming against our kingdom. The psychiatrists are ours! We know they accomplish nothing, but the people don't know it.

"You are supposed to be scared. We keep coming against you, and you won't stop. She's just like you; she won't stop. She's helping you, Roy. We've got to stop you."

Changing the subject, the demon continued. "I am hungry! I'm hungry! I'm hungry! Get me some food. We like to eat. We have desires just like you do. We have likes and dislikes. We like to talk, that's why we go to the psychiatrists, the stupid fools! We talk all the time, but we want to hear someone talk to us. That is why we send patients to the psychiatrists. They talk back to us. They think they are talking to the patients. Then we get angry and go berserk. The psychiatrist thinks it's the patients."

Realizing the demons were telling the truth, Bishop Bryant quickly reminded them of the reason they were now here in the Bible Church of Christ.

"We cast out evil spirits."

Angrily the demons screamed, "It's us! It's us! You don't have to drive us out. All you have to do is leave us alone!"

As Bishop Bryant continued to pray, the demon continued to give us his message. "I am the god of this world. You are coming against our kingdom."

Soon I began to cough up the phlegm and lost the demon.

Bishop Bryant identified the demon of Lying.

Crying out in rage, the demon screamed, "Don't tell her that! You'll destroy us!:

I heard Bishop Bryant telling me to hate the lying demons. They had lied to me all along. I began to have hope and encouragement as the demons revealed their plans in their boasts and complaints.

"You are messing up our work. Why did you do that? Now you've told her how to close the door." A closed door meant the demons could not return. "We saw her. **We** knew where she was going. She didn't even know. Satan said to stop her. You've done too much. You've made Jezebel beg. No one makes Jezebel beg. You've made **Pride** humble himself. Your head is hard as rock. You won't believe anything. That's why you don't have any friends in the ministry. You won't give up, and you won't shut up."

Bishop Bryant told the demon that his friend was Jesus. The demon hated to hear that, because he cried out, "Don't tell me that! I don't want to hear that. You need friends in the ministry to back you up. Where are they? They are all somewhere laughing at you. They say this is a demon church. Do you know how many ministers are compromising with us, but you won't compromise. Your church could be filled with people, Roy, if you could just compromise. Leave us alone, and we will send you the people. We will set you up pretty."

Bishop Bryant began to cite to the demon the Scripture where Jesus was offered the kingdom of this world in Luke 4:5-10:

"Again, the devil taketh him (Jesus) up into an exceeding high mountain, and sheweth him all the kingdoms of the world, and the glory of them; And saith unto him, 'All these things will I give thee, if thou wilt fall down and worship me.' Then saith Jesus unto him, 'Get thee hence, Satan: for it is written, Thou shalt worship the Lord thy God and him only shalt thou serve.' The devil leaveth him, and behold, angels came and ministered unto him."

The demon of Lies cried out, "I don't want to hear that. You need carpet, Roy, in Monticello, and Mount Vernon (two church sites). We can give you gold and carpeting; we'll set you up. Teach the people about the Holy Ghost, fine. Just leave deliverance alone. We see the people coming. You are not supposed to have anyone on your side. Satan told us to take all your people, all the people who love you. He said to go through the ministry and destroy the children."

As Corrupt Communication withdrew, Hatred of Men manifested again. "We are taking her into her childhood. We take the patients into their childhoods, and then allow the psychiatrist to bring them back. Explain to your people, Roy, why she's not coming back. She is now a twelve year old. She is not going to tell anybody anything. How can a child tell them anything?"

I felt myself take on the characteristics of a twelve year old. I vividly recalled my own voice at that age.

Hatred of Men began speaking again. "Everybody knows Toni. She is now a little girl and I am not bringing her back. What is going to happen to your deliverance ministry now? Take her to the psychiatrist."

Bishop Bryant informed the demons he was only allowing the demons to talk at such length because everything was being recorded.

"I don't care," said Hated of Men. "That tape is not going to mean anything when you have to explain why Toni is twelve years old. Take her to a mental institution. They will dope her up, but we like medicine. They give us pills and injections. They bomb us out. We get tired; we rest. Then they think the patient is all right. We are just quiet because we are bombed out of our skulls. We like to get high.

"I told you, Roy, we like to eat. Some people feed us garbage, but we like to eat. We like to take pills. Who do you think does these things? It's is not the patients. It's us.

"You are telling too much, Roy Bryant. The people are finding out there is no hope in the psychiatry business. You are not supposed to do that. We are making billions of dollars off these suckers, and you are spoilng it. You are giving away valuable information. There is no cure for the mentally ill. Let them believe that. You are bringing destruction. Leave us alone! Don't write it! Don't tell it! Don't put anymore of these testimonies on the radio and TV. Don't do anything. We will set you up pretty. You will have nothing to worry about. We will fill your churches. What about Jamaica? We'll send clothes to your church in Jamaica.

"Let it go and we will give you Toni back. You won't have to explain anything. She'll be here Sunday mornings teaching Sunday School. Let her go. We won't take her right away."

Bishop Bryant began to preach love to the demon of Hatred of Men. He told him the church loved me, and the Lord loved me. The demon could not stand love; he became angry.

148

"Do you see this cross, demon?" asked Bishop Bryant. "I hate the cross. I hate the blood... I hate it."

Bishop Bryant began to quote the Word. "John 14:12: He that believeth on me, the works that I do shall he do also; and greater works than these shall he do; because I go unto the Father."

Angrily the demon replied, "That's what's wrong with this church, too much Word. I hate the Word. Why don't you go into politics?"

"You are our politics," answered Bishop Bryant.

"But I have to sit and listen to the Word of God over and over again," the demon whined. "It cuts me and torments me."

The demon was telling the truth. I love the Word of God, and I sat under Bishop Bryant's teaching and preaching as often as I could. If I was in church listening, so were the demons within me. They heard as much of the Word of God as I did. I enjoyed it, but they hated it.

Bishop Bryant invited him to leave, but the demon protested that he had to stay. "We've got to give you credit, Roy, you can really preach the Word, but people don't listen. It goes in one ear and out the other. We are doing a booming business, because of the people's disobedience. People don't listen; they are hard-headed. When they disobey, we step in. Churches are full of hard-headed people.

"Young people don't obey their parents; we are taking the young people one by one. Kids talk back; they are smoking and having sex. They do exactly what they want to do, but they are turning their backs on pastors, parents and Sunday School teachers.

"Why do you think there are problems in the churches? We hear you talking to them. While you are talking, we are talking. They think we are their own thoughts. We're taking them out of the churches. These little brats don't want to obey. We hate them.

"Toni is talking to the children, telling them about us. She's telling them they are not too young for the devil to use them. We've got to stop her. The youth are going to die. We have to kill off the youth; we have to kill them all. We are going to keep them from the deliverance ministry. Then we'll attack the strong saints. This is war!"

During all the threats Bishop Bryant continued to pray. He recorded the demons speaking in order to reveal their perverseness, hatred for mankind, and their plans.

"The blood of Jesus. Look at the cross of Calvary. In the name of Jesus." Bishop Bryant pounded into the demon verbally. As I began to cough the phlegm was released. Bishop Bryant and Mother Bryant continued praying. "Come out of her mind, out of her sexual organs. Come out of her in the name of Jesus Christ." The demons could stand no more. They began to accuse Bishop Bryant of burning them. They were truthful. They were burning with the Holy Ghost anointing.

As the demon of Hatred of Men withdrew, Corrupt Communication came forth cursing. I could feel myself changing personalities almost as easily as changing a pair of shoes. Corrupt Communication informed Bishop Bryant that people hated him. Bishop Bryant's answer was that people loved him also. The demon could not deal with love. The demon began to plead for mercy.

I felt the demons had nerve to ask for mercy; they had none on me. They had just boasted that they hated mankind. Instead of extending mercy, Bishop demanded that he leave my throat and lose my tongue.

"This is my home. The voice box is mine," the demon cried. He had inadvertently disclosed his hiding place. "Me and my big mouth. I don't know when to shut up."

Now that we had identified him and his dwelling, his hold was weakened on me. Self-destruction, Self-devaluation, Memory, Childhood Rape, and others began crying with loud voices. It reminded me of Acts 8:5-8.

"Then Philip went down to the city of Samaria, and preached Christ unto them. And the people with one accord gave heed unto those things which Philip spake, hearing and seeing the miracles which h e did. For unclean Spirits, crying with loud voice, came out of many that were possessed with them; and many taken with palsies, and that were lame, were healed. And there was great joy in that city."

There was now great joy in the Bible Church of Christ. I was being delivered from numerous spirits. Immediately after I was free from these, Bishop Bryant began to attack Hatred of Men. He commanded him to come out from the ear gate, the mind, the thought life, and my whole body. The time for talking was ended.

Hatred of Men came forth hollering, "No! No! I have to hate! I have to work." His work was finished. Hatred of Men was expelled, and I began to praise God. I had a great joy in my soul, like that in the city of Samaria.

Bishop Bryant asked me how I felt, if I was willing to keep battling. "I want to go after Corrupt Communication, Toni."

In total agreement I said, "I feel great. I'm being set free. Let's see if he's gone."

Bishop Bryant laid his hands on me and commanded that Corrupt Communication manifest himself. He came forth cursing and screaming. He was angry that I was writing Christian material; he wanted me to write for the demons.

"Write for you, demons? That is an insult!" declared Bishop Bryant. "You will have her writing garbage."

"That's right. She can write for *True Confessions*, *Secrets*, and other publications. After the demon finished outlining his plans, I began to go to sleep. I could only faintly hear Bishop Bryant because of the sudden tiredness that overcame me. In the middle of a deliverance I was falling asleep. Mother Bryant began to call out Sleepiness, Slumber and Tiredness. Immediately my body began to jerk. I yawned uncontrollably while they called the demons out in the name of Jesus. Instantly I was awake again.

Corrupt Communication surfaced as soon as I lost the demons of Sleepiness and Tiredness. He was angrier than ever.

"You've done enough work for today. You've done too much. Look at what you are doing to her. You are destroying our work. We are supposed to kill her; I'm sick of you! I am not coming out of here. We've got work to do. You don't listen. Your head is as hard as a rock. We see the people coming. You are drawing people. We see it; leave it alone. People are beginning to believe. They are coming to see. Stop it!"

After his tirade Bishop Bryant calmly asked him if he was finished.

"Get your hands off her voice box," was the demon's only reply.

Bishop Bryant began to call on the name of Jesus.

The demon went into a rage. "Don't call that name! I hate that name! If you don't get your hands off her voice box, I'll rip out her throat! She'll never say another word."

"No, you won't," Bishop Bryant calmly replied. "I bind you in the name of Jesus. Now come out of her."

Corrupt Communication kept babbling, giving away valuable information which actually helped us in the deliverance, especially the statement that I was dirty.

"She's clean. She's been cleansed by the Word of God," replied Bishop Bryant.

Suddenly a demon screamed, "Why did you tell her that? Now she knows the truth."

Using the gift of discernment, Bishop Bryant realized the spirit's name was Uncleanness. I heard a hideous scream and a plea for mercy come from my own mouth. The demon of Uncleanness called for his master, Satan, to help.

"Please, Satan, where are you? Don't leave me, Master. Come help me! Where is my master? I am going to tell Satan on you, Roy Bryant. I am going to tell what you are doing to me. I've been in her so long. All these years she's been mine. Help me, Satan!"

The demon screamed an incredible and sorrowful wail. Had it not been an evil spirit, I might have felt sorry for him. But I was too happy to be finally clean. After coughing I was again bathed in praise, as I had been after each deliverance. Twenty-two years of believing I was unclean had taken its toll on me, but I felt God's restoration beginning immediately.

Corrupt Communication was not happy about my condition. His anger seemed to have tripled.

"Now you've done it. You've destroyed the pillar in here. He was the strong man. We were set up so well in here. Now we're in trouble because of you, but you are not getting rid of me.

"Nobody will believe you. You are a weirdo, and she is just like you! I don't like you, Roy Bryant. You are hardheaded, and you just don't quit. I hate hardheaded people! I am not hardheaded; I have been sent to bring you down, and I am doing my work."

Bishop Bryant countered that he was also doing his work, and he was sent to free people of demonic oppression and possession. Missionary Mary Smith Parker began to read the Bible in the hearing of Corrupt Communication. After a period of time I began to cough and expel the demon. I had successfully been delivered of Self-Devaluation, Self-Destruction, Hatred of Men, Sleepiness, Tiredness, False Marriage, Uncleanness, and Corrupt Communication. Hallelujah!

XV

DEMONS SPEAKING # 3

"Here we go again! You're not searching me!" the demon exclaimed. "Get out of here and leave my ears alone! My name is False Prophet, and I've been quiet long enough! That man (referring to Jesus) won't let me work. I was going to destroy her and that gift, but that man won't let me do my job. Why should I be in here if I can't work? I've got to discredit her. I've got to close the people's ears to her. Her testimony is too powerful. They watch and believe her. I understand that your Jesus is cleaning house today. There are six of us in here, besides me. You won't get all of us today. It's not going to be easy. You want her? I'm going to make you work for her!"

We were in the middle of another deliverance session. When False Prophet finished his speech, Bishop Bryant laid his hands upon me and the anointing burned the demon.

"You are not going into anyone else in this room. I am binding your powers," stated Bishop. "Come out in the name of Jesus." I began to cough and release the mucus. Joy began to bubble up in me. In a matter of minutes I was free. I loved to hear Bishop Bryant boast in the cross of Jesus Christ.

"Where did False Prophet go?" I asked. "He said he was going to make me work." I had a good laugh at that.

In the middle of my laughter an angry voice said, "I am going to kill her! She can't eat anything. Ask her when she ate last. She is hungry and she can't eat. She is going to starve. She looks at food and can't eat it. Tables of food are in front of her, but she isn't able to touch a bite." The demon was telling the truth; he had again turned off my appetite.

"Toni will eat tonight, Undereating demon. I am going to burn you up and out of her. You are to come out of her mouth and from her taste buds," Bishop Bryant commanded.

"I want a home, Roy Bryant! Either give me a home, or I'll take your appetite," replied the demon.

"You don't have enough power to take my appetite, Undereating. Now tell me how you reentered Toni's body."

Without hesitation, Undereating, described his open door. "We lied to her. She thought God wanted her to fast. We told her God had given her grace to fast. We had to get back in some way. She fasted for three days, but stopped short of five because you told her to eat. You told her God wasn't talking to her about fasting.

"We could have taken the flesh off her bones. We were closing her appetite completely until you returned from Hawaii. You always come back at the wrong time. You are messing up our work. They need you in Hawaii.

"From the beginning you have messed us up. We had her mind. Now she has a strong mind, and it's your fault. You people don't know how to eat. You either overeat and undereat. You are not going to expel me, Roy Bryant. I will brace myself."

Bishop Bryant quietly called Undereating out, along with Underweight, in the name of Jesus.

"You were enough trouble, Roy Bryant, all by yourself. You have brought destruction upon us. Why did He (Jesus) have to send her here? She was ours. Look at what she's doing; she won't shut up. Stop these testimonies."

"Undereating, I've only let you speak to reveal your character. Now you may no longer speak," commanded Bishop. "Come out of the taste buds and bring your friends with you. The blood of Jesus is against you. Come out of the legs, the buttocks, the arms, the thighs." When he mentioned my legs, they began to run at an incredible speed, although I was sitting.

In the midst of the running, I heard "Get your hands off my legs! These are my legs! Leave them alone! They're skinny legs." Soon the pleading and running was replaced by my own praises. I was free!

"How do you feel, Toni?" Bishop Bryant asked.

"I feel fine, Bishop. I feel good! I feel great!"

As I rejoiced, a lying demon surfaced. "Toni wants to sing. She has to go to choir rehearsal tonight." The lying demon was using the truth to end this deliverance session.

"Since Toni has choir practice, I must get you out of her in a few seconds," countered Bishop.

"Oh, shut up! Logic! Where did you get all that logic?" the demon angrily retorted. "Where did you get all those words? You have an answer for everything. Every time she comes to you, you have something to tell her! We can't hide in here anymore. I'm tired of you and your words."

"We have two minutes left to get you out," repeated Bishop. "I know where you are. You are a lying demon in her voice box."

"That's right," said Liar, "I am in the voice box. I am not a lying demon; I am a liar. I don't like the word demon. When you say "demon," people think we are nasty. Don't say it that way. I am not a demon; I am a liar!"

"Do you have any last words?" Bishop asked him.

No answer, but quietly I heard him say "I am not a demon."

"No last words, except you are not a demon." I wondered how Bishop Bryant had heard him. "Then what are you?" he continued.

"I am a spirit!" The demon began to whine. "Now you've told her everything; she's wise to us. We'll have to pay. She even told her mother the truth this week." Earlier that week I had confessed everything I had hidden for twenty-two years to my mother, so the demons would have nothing to hold over me. I wanted nothing hidden any longer.

Liar continued to cry, "I hate the truth."

"You hate the truth, Liar, because Jesus is the Truth," Bishop replied.

The demon began to lie. "We don't do those things you say. We hear you all the time. We are not demons."

"That's the biggest lie you've ever told, Lying Demon! See the blood? Every time I say the 'blood of Jesus,' I feel so good. Now come out of her, you liar."

"I hate this body anyhow! I am going where I am free to work. I'm coming out, but I am taking my time." Liar left crying in a loud voice. "I can't stand the blood. It is life. Don't say 'the blood.' You make a nervous wreck of me, Roy Bryant!" I heard the demon screaming for Satan's help. "Master, Master! Help me. Don't leave me. Don't leave me on my own like this."

My freedom brought joy, and the joy caused me to praise God. I could hear Bishop calling the demon by name, but I knew I was free. Bishop Bryant realized it too. "Liar is gone. Undereating and Underweight are gone False Prophet is gone.

"What about Corrupt Communication? Where are you? Come out from the ear gate, from the voice box!" I was relieved to hear Bishop Bryant command this demon to leave. In every deliverance the cursing had dominated my speech. I knew it was more than the nature of the demons, especially from the activity of my thought life. He had also

158

withdrawn to let another demon surface in several deliverances. In our efforts to identify more damaging demons, we had omitted this one.

Corrupt Communication came forth this time cursing and threatening to rip my voice box, so that I could never speak another word.

"You are cursing because you know I am going to burn you," stated Bishop.

"Oh no, me and my big mouth! I can never shut up! That's my problem."

"Father, in the name of Jesus Christ of Nazareth, I call this Corrupt Communication demon out of the body."

After a period of silence, the demon spoke. "I am resting."

"You are not resting," stated Bishop. "I just spoke the word and I know what is happening to you. You can fool someone else; you are not fooling me. Why are you spitting if you are resting?" I was spitting phlegm into paper towels.

Corrupt Communication admitted, "You are breaking me up. You know what you are doing to me."

Bishop Bryant continued to minister, and Corrupt Communication began to scream for mercy. "Please give me another chance; I will be quiet." (This was against his nature) "Leave my ears alone. She is not going to let me back in. She has become wise to me. I heard her talking. Please! First give me a home. You have plenty of words. Give me a home. You have the power to give me a home, and you know it."

"I have the power to give you a home, but I am going to send you out of this building into the dogs."

"I can't talk in no dog! I don't want no dog!" yelled the demon. "That's as bad as swine." The demon was referring to the incident recorded in Mark, chapter 5, where Jesus delivered the Gadarene Demoniac from thousands of demons and sent them into a herd of pigs when the demons

159

pleaded with Him. The pigs had run to their deaths over a cliff when the demons entered them.

"They were left without a home," the demon screamed. "I don't want to talk about that. I am not going into the dogs. I don't want to bark the rest of my life. I can't enjoy myself in a dog. Give me a body. Give me somebody."

"No," replied Bishop, "I am not going to give you any body. God loves his people, and He also loves the sinner. Therefore, I am not sending you into any body." Inside I felt like giggling at the desperation of the demon, although he was using my voice for his speech.

"If you send me into the dogs, I'll come back and bite you. That will fix you!" Giggles broke from my mouth at that thought. "It's not funny. I am going to bite you. It will serve you right," the demon exclaimed.

Calmly Bishop reminded him that he had power over dogs. "Remember the pack of dogs that came toward me some years ago?"

"Don't remind me," screamed the demon.

"Where were you then?" Bishop asked. "They thought they were going to have me for dinner. They turned and went the other way when I called on the name of Jesus.

"Corrupt Communication, you can no longer stay. Leave the ear gate and the ears. We clean the ears in the name of Jesus. The blood of Jesus is against you. Get out of the ear gate, out of the voice box."

Miraculously Corrupt Communication was expelled and I began to praise God. I heard Bishop counting.

"That's five gone. Sexual Lust is number six."

At the mention of lust, I felt my body sliding off the chair and the desire to run. Fearing she was about to be defeated, Sexual Lust made her intentions known.

"I've been here too long. I am the only way we can destroy her now. I will destroy her anointing. I know what she came to do. I can separate her from the Christ. She's got to be a clean vessel to belong to Him."

Bishop Bryant continued to minister, praying in tongues and quoting scripture. Lust continued to cry. "No! I was born in here. She has power. This is our last chance. She's going to look good. I will use her. I am the last hope."

"Toni hates you," Bishop stated.

"Maybe she does now, but she'll change her mind. She hasn't done anything so far, but I'm patient. She likes to live holy now; there's no sense in a woman like this. Sex is important. She has to have it. She's denying herself for that man." Lust tried to be convincing.

"Call that man, Jesus," said Bishop. "His name is Jesus."

Angrily, Lust screamed, "Don't call his name! She's clean; she's pure. Let me use her. I'm the best friend she's ever had. She used to like me." Without any mercy, Bishop Bryant called Lust out of every part of my body, and he included Fantasy again just in case. I was set free.

As soon as I began to praise God my tongue went rigid as a board. It began to dart around inside and outside my mouth like a snake thrusts its tongue. It was a demon I had not expected: Oral Sex.

"I am not working!" he screamed. "Don't bother me! Leave me alone! I am not making her do anything. I won't use her, I promise. Don't make me leave, please!" I could feel Oral Sex on my tongue, inside my mouth and jaws as he whined and pleaded for a home. The word of God released me from that demon also.

Another demon began to speak. "My name is Masturbation. Leave me alone. I am not working. Why bother me? It is not my time." Bishop cast him from my body also.

All I could say was "Hallelujah, he's gone!"

"How do you feel, Toni? How many was that?"

I couldn't help but smile. "I feel fine, Bishop, but there is another. His name is Self-rejection."

161

As soon as we identified him, he began to holler, "Her father rejected her. She was bad. He did it. She's rejecting herself. I made her believe she was a nobody. I was doing a good job. She is a nobody. If she ever finds out who she is, she will mess us up."

"Out, Self-rejection! Bring your nest with you. This is your last chance. Today, February 24, 1983, you are coming out by the blood of Jesus," Bishop commanded.

"You are tearing my roots, Roy Bryant! Where will I go? For nineteen years this has been my home." I heard a high-pitched wail from my own mouth and then silence. He too lost his home.

God blessed Bishop to deliver me from nine demons in just a matter of hours. "For no man can do these miracles that thou doest, except God be with him," John 3:2.

"How do you feel, Toni?"

"I feel fine, Bishop Bryant. I'm tired but happy to be free. Thank you."

XVI

DELIVERANCE PRAYER BREAKFAST

Three hundred people filled the main dining room for the deliverance prayer breakfast at the Bible Church of Christ in Mount Vernon. The people gathered at 9:30 on that Saturday morning, not just for breakfast, but also for deliverance from all types of evil spirits.

At the Bible Church we took seriously the scripture in Matthew 10:8 "Cast out devils: freely ye have received, freely give." I especially liked that it was indeed a Bible church, and I have never been charged a fee for any deliverance or ministry I have received. The work in these sessions is often tedious and tiresome, but all is done in love for souls, and to the glory of God. Men and women ordained by God worked with me and others in the services out of love for the body of Christ.

This prayer breakfast also provided fellowship with one another. We ate together, praised God together, and sang along with the Bible Church of Christ Mount Vernon Male Chorus. After the breakfast and singing, Bishop Bryant taught a lesson that was always lengthy, yet informative. No two sessions were the same. The Holy Spirit knew who needed what, when and how. The Spirit of God put His finger on my problems, and those of others too, through the pastor's message. That message was always simple, but direct, and diagrams such as the

Hammonds' drawing of the hands in *Pigs in the Parlor* were used to explain the identity and activity of demons.

I could barely wait for the teaching to end. I was there to lose the Spirit of Adultery, so I did not hesitate to take the paper towels offered. I expected to be delivered. Before the prayer began, I was asked to testify before the assembly. Testifying meant glorifying God, and freedom for other souls. I was aware that someone else present had the same problems that I had experienced. If my testimony helped set someone else free, it was a small price to pay, because giving a testimony was hard. I had to speak of the filth of Satan in my life, but I was also uncovering the work of evil spirits. I did not intend to hurt souls who had come to be blessed.

At the conclusion of my testimony I told the congregation that I was going for broke today. I wanted every demon out of me. I was especially angry with the Spirit of Adultery. The teaching and testimonies left the demons exposed. The results were up to the individuals in the congregation. How desperate were we to receive our deliverance? I looked around to see if Satan had fanned anyone to sleep and found we were all holding on.

Although I desired to pray for others' deliverances, I knew I needed to receive ministry first and then work if time allowed. By now I was also casting out evil spirits by the authority of Jesus Christ. That authority was not given to ministers only, but to all Spirit-filled believers in Christ. It is written, "These signs shall follow them that believe; In my name (Jesus) shall they cast out devils," Mark 16;17.

Bishop Bryant began to pray. We were instructed how to renounce Satan and his demons. We hated him and his demons. First Bishop Bryant called out Telephone Spirit. Just as I expected, I had an immediate reaction. A demon had entered me by the telephone. The only open door I knew existed was in my childhood, at the age of eight or nine. I had picked up the phone and cursed the operator with my four letter words. Satan took advantage of the opportunity and the demon made his home in me.

I have since learned that the telephone is not a place to carry on corrupt communication. Demons of sexual lust and other types of perverted spirits enter by that avenue. We need to be careful of what we hear, and who is talking in our ear, and what the source is. When I was delivered from the Telephone Spirit that day, I began to guard my ears.

I was quickly delivered of the demon of Curse Inheritance. The Spirit of Adultery followed, crying with a loud voice, "I was born in here. This has been my home for thirty years."

I was able to relax for a fraction of a second before the Spirit of Backsliding manifested. I heard him proclaiming loudly, "I was not coming back to church!" The unpleasant truth is that not all who backslide necessarily want to do so.

Suddenly I was plunged into darkness. My body grew weaker and weaker. I explained to the Elder, the young elder ministering the deliverance to me, what was happening; he called out the Spirit of Weakness. As it left I was strengthened physically, mentally, and spiritually, all at the same time.

Soon my fists became clenched just as they had in the hotel room with Mr. Lee twenty-two years ago. Murder was manifesting himself in my hands. Greater than the threats pouring from my mouth was the word of God. As the people ministering deliverance spoke the commandment "Thou shalt not kill," I began to feel the demon releasing my hands and my mind. The deliverance brought relief, but the pit of darkness engulfed me again.

I felt maggots, slime, and worms traveling from one area of my body to another, which created an uncontrollable itching in my legs, my arms, my ears, and on my chest. It was the Spirit of Insecurity, and then a Boyfriend spirit. Insecurity was cast out, and Wil came forward. Satan said I had only one choice, go back to the old boyfriend, Wil. The demon in me would help me make that choice.

Satan lied. I had two choices, and I chose Jesus. The same Holy Ghost, who broke the yoke the first time, did it again in deliverance. Jesus came to my defense.

Demons tried to gain complete control of my thoughts. The only thing I understood was that I had to continue to fight. My thoughts were confused and incoherent. After a period of time, I could no longer discern who was speaking. All I could do was let words come forth.

"Please, no more deliverance! I want to go home, now! This life is too hard. I am going through too much. I am never going to be free. I want to be left alone so I can end it all." Although I verbalized these thoughts to the Elder, he ignored them and continued to minister deliverance to me.

"That's not you, Toni. Someone else is speaking."

I became angry. "I want to go home. I am going to kill myself."

Suicide manifested himself. Later I thanked the man of God who was able to discern the voice of the demon from my own. Identification of the demon encouraged us. By three a.m. I had been set free of eight demons. My body felt slightly bruised; my throat was sore; but I was free. At ten a.m. the next morning I sat in my Sunday School class, tired and rejoicing.

I have lost a total of forty-three demons since I became a Christian. The scripture in I John 4:4 is fulfilled in my life. "Ye are of God, little children, and have overcome them: because greater is he (the Holy Ghost) that is in you, than he that is in the world (Satan)."

XVII

APPLE IN THE TOP OF THE TREE

"He found him in a desert land, and in the waste howling wilderness, he (Jesus) led him about, he instructed him, he kept him as the apple of his eye,"

Deut. 32:10.

"The Spirit of the Lord God is upon me; because the Lord hath anointed me to preach good tidings unto the meek; he hath sent me to bind up the broken-hearted, to proclaim liberty to the captives, and the opening of the prison to them that are bound,"

Isaiah 61:1.

"I will greatly rejoice in the Lord, my soul shall be joyful in my God; for he hath covered me with the garments of salvation, he hath covered me with the robe of righteousness, as a bridegroom decketh himself with ornaments, and as a bride adorneth herself with her jewels,"

Isaiah 61:10.

Hello, world! Look at me now! The Lord has taken pleasure in me. He has beautified me with salvation. Therefore, the high praise of God is in my mouth and a two-edged sword is in my hand. What I've seen, I've written. The testimony of God's anointed is now binding up and healing the broken-hearted. His gifts of writing and speaking are being used to proclaim liberty to those that have been held captive for years by Satan. The same are now walking away, freed from prisons of sin and destruction. I can't help but rejoice in the God of my salvation.

I have found my place again in the top of the tree, hanging high and proud for all the world to see. This tree reaches òut with loving arms and protects me from the evil of this world. I am nestled safely in it arms, growing in the love and grace of Jesus Christ. It is only now that I completely understand the protection of this magnificent tree. Before I was old enough to appreciate the parable of the apple in the tree, Satan stole it from me. Because of deliverance I have gained the loving memory, and the revelation and understanding of what I was taught as a child.

The apple in the top of the tree was meant to be a special fruit, as "children are the fruit of the womb." My fruits are the deeds done in my body and the works which I manifest. I have advanced beyond the child-like parable of an apple to possession of the nine fruit of the Spirit. I am the apple of my Lord's eye, identified by love, joy, peace, longsuffering, gentleness, goodness, faith, meekness, and temperance. Possession and identification came by the Holy Ghost. Matthew 7:20 says, "Wherefore by their fruits ye shall know them."

According to John 15:1-2 Jesus said, "I am the true vine and my Father is the husbandman. Every branch in me that beareth not fruit, he taketh away: and every branch that beareth fruit, he purgeth it, that it bring forth more fruit." No corrupt tree can bring forth good fruit. Neither can a good tree bring forth corrupt fruit. Matthew 12:33 says, "The tree is known by its fruit."

I am the fruit of the labor of the Bible Church of Christ. I have been restored to the top because God placed me in a ministry second to none. Jesus said, "Abide in me and I in you. As the branch cannot bear fruit of itself, except it abide in the vine, no more can ye, except ye abide in me. I am the vine and ye are the branches. He that abideth in me, and I in him, the same bringeth forth much fruit." John 15:4-8. Nothing can prevent me from bringing forth fruit up to a hundredfold. This book is just one of the fruits of my labor. All who read and believe can be totally delivered.

My deliverance brought graduation from business school. It freed me from poverty and welfare and enabled me to support myself. It is knowing that God will supply every need. Deliverance has meant hair growth and weight gain. It has meant bodily strength and mental alertness. It has brought me joy beyond my expectations and knowledge beyond a secular education. Deliverance has brought complete freedom from abnormal and perverse thoughts, voices and actions, and an end to psychiatric evaluations and medication.

I give thanks to a wonderful mom and dad who "trained me up in the way I should go." Thanks also to the Bible Church of Christ, Bishop Roy Bryant, Sr., and mother Sissieretta Bryant, who stood steadfast with me.

My purpose in life has been fulfilled. I am an ordained evangelist in the Bible Church of Christ ministry. To God be the glory! I am preaching, teaching, and exercising my gifts of laying on of hands for the baptism of the Holy Ghost, casting out demons, and healings. I am a deliverance minister, street preacher, subway preacher, jailhouse preacher, and teacher. I have earned a Bachelor's Degree in Theology and currently am working toward a Master's Degree.

Thousands have heard my testimony by radio, television, and print. My testimony is only a fraction of what has been done for many through the ministry of the Bible Church of Christ. Some will never tell it. Others have moved on, but the fruit of the labor of this ministry will remain until the day of the Lord, and throughout eternity. It is a strong, powerful representation of the entire works of Jesus Christ. We are "encompassed by a great cloud of witnesses" as is written in the book of Hebrews.

Remember, deliverance or psychiatry, the choice is yours.

PASTOR'S ENDORSEMENT

Greetings, in the name of our Lord and Savior Jesus Christ.

It gives me great pleasure to endorse this book. It is especially pleasurable since I was the instrument which God used to deliver the sweet soul of Antoinette Cannaday.

As a minister of the Gospel of Jesus Christ, having been in the deliverance ministry, and dealing in demonology, from the beginning of my calling in 1959, I have seen thousands of souls set free in Africa, the West Indies and other parts of the world, where I have labored in deliverance.

Antoinette came into our church in a state I wouldn't care to describe. She was in the worst condition, spiritually, I have ever seen in anyone. Her deliverance boiled down to a test of wills. I was determined against all opposition that warred against my patience to see her set free.

Now as to the results: After each deliverance session, I saw her open up like a flower springing up in a garden. You watch as a plant begins to grow and then rejoice to see the flower come forth. In the last deliverance session, Antoinette opened up like a beautiful rose of Sharon. God is moving powerfully in her life, not only in testifying, but Antoinette has also become a very capable minister in our ministry.

This book, *Out Of Me Went 43 Demons,* is true, every word of it. In fact, we could not include every part of Antoinette's story, but we have given enough to show that the God of Heaven still rules in the kingdoms of men.

With all my heart I pray that through this book, God might encourage those of you who are in the deliverance ministry, and might also help those seeking deliverance to find it.

Bishop Roy Bryant, Sr., D.D.
Pastor of The Bible Churches of Christ, Inc.

THE BIBLE CHURCH OF CHRIST, INC.
BISHOP ROY BRYANT, SR., D.D. PASTOR AND FOUNDER
Website: www.thebiblechurchofchrist.org

1358 Morris Ave.	1069 Morris Ave.	100 W. 2nd St.
Bronx, NY 10456	Bronx, NY 10456	Mt. Vernon, NY 10550
(718) 588-2284	(718) 992-4653	(914) 664- 4602

1132 Congress St.	512 W. Vernon St.	Diamond Acres
Schenectady, NY 12302	Kinston, NC 28502	Dagsboro, DE19939
(518) 382-5625	(252) 527-7739	(302) 732-3351

1-J Diamond Ruby
St. Croix, Virgin Islands
(340) 779-3268

THE BIBLE CHURCH OF CHRIST, INC.
Lingumpally, Hyderabad, India

THE BIBLE CHURCH OF CHRIST THEOLOGICAL INSTITUTE
Dr. Roy Bryant, Sr., President
Dr. Alice Jones, Dean

1358 Morris Avenue (nr. 170th St)	100 West Second St.
Bronx, NY 10456	Mount Vernon, NY 10550
(718) 588-2284	(914) 664-4602
Fax (718) 992-5597	Fax (914) 668-6778

Diamond Acres	I-J Diamond Ruby
Dagsboro, DE 19939	St. Croix, Virgin Island
(302) 732-3351	(304)779-3268

courses offered:
New Converts, Christian Workers, Evangelism, General Bible, Teachers'
Training, Post Graduate in Theology, Advanced Pedagogy, Spanish,
GED Classes, Youth Expressions, Josephus, and more
For those interested in learning the ministry of **Demonology**, Bishop Roy
Bryant, Sr. DD assisted By Evangelist Antoinette Cannaday are
conducting classes in our Theological Institute. Please call our Institute
@ (914) 664-4602 for further information.

THE BIBLE CHURCH OF CHRIST CHRISTIAN BOOKSTORE

1358 Morris Avenue (nr. 170th St.)

Bronx, NY 10456

(718) 293-1928

We carry a large selection of books, Bibles, Clery attire (including robes), tapes, CD's certificate, Sunday School Supplies, Gifts and much, much more.

DEMONOLOGY TAPES
BY BISHOP ROY BRYANT, SR. D.D.

SATAN THE MOTIVATOR
2 TAPE TEACHING SERIES

HOW TO EXPELL DEMONS FROM HOME
(BISHOP BRYANT EXPELLS THE DEMONS FROM YOUR HOUSE)

SELF-DELIVERANCE TAPE
(RECEIVE YOUR OWN DELIVERANCE IN THE PRIVACY OF YOUR HOME)

WHO'S IN YOUR BODY WITH YOU?
(SIX-TAPE DELIVERANCE/TEACHING SERIES)

DEMONS SPEAKING #1, #2, #3
(THE PRIVATE DELIVERANCE OF ANTOINETTE CANNADAY)

DEMONS SPEAKING #4
PRIVATE DELIVERANCE SESSION OF ONE YOUNG LADY

THE MINISTER IN DISTRESS
AN ELDER OF THE GOSPEL DELIVERED FROM HOMOSEXUALITY

THE EXORCIST CAST OUT 15 DEMONS – 2 TAPE SERIES
LEARN HOW THE EXORCIST CASTS OUT DEMONS IN A INDIVIDUAL

HOW TO CAST OUT DEMONS – 2 TAPE SERIES
TEACHING SERIES WHICH WILL TAKE YOU FROM THE BEGINNING TO THE ENDING OF THE BIBLE IDENTIFYING THE WORKS OF SATAN.

DEMONOLGY TEACHING TAPES
BY EVANGELIST ANTOINETTE CANNADAY

I HAVE BEEN DELIVERED, NOW WHAT?
(HOW TO CLOSE THE DOOR ON DEMONS TO KEEP YOUR
DELIVERANCE)

HOW DO I KNOW IF I NEED DELIVERANCE?
(IS IT THE WORKS OF THE FLESH OR IS IT DEMONIC?)

THE ABUSED WOMEN IN CHURCH – NOT FOR WOMEN ONLY
(HOW TO IDENTIFY AND RECORNIZE ABUSE IN ANY FORM)

THE BATTLE WITHIN
(RECOGNIZE DEMONS WITHIN AND DEMONS WITHOUT)
DEMONONOLGY WOMEN CONFERENCES -
$24.00 A SET ($6 each)
EACH CONFERENCES ARE FOUR-TAPE SERIES – SATURDAY,
2000 TAPE #2 SIDE 2 INCLUDES A PERSONAL/SELF .
DELIVERANCE SESSION. LADIES BE DELIVERED IN THE
PRIVACY OF YOUR OWN HOME.

Current price for each tape is $6.00. Please included 1.50 for shipping
and handling. For multiple tapes, please send $3.20 for priority mailing.

Other books in the ministry of The Bible Church of Christ

MANUAL ON DEMONOLOGY, DIARY OF AN EXORCIST
SATAN THE MOTIVATOR, THE BATTLE BETWEEN GOD AND SATAN
WHO'S IN YOUR BODY WITH YOU – WORKBOOK
BY BISHOP ROY BRYANT, SR., D.D.
CURRENT PRICE $19.95 EA.

READ THE POWERFUL TESTIMONY OF DELIVERANCE FROM HOMOSEXUALITY
"SILENCE EQUALS DEATH, EXPOSING THE DEEDS OF DARKNESS"
BY SISTER RETTIE WINFIELD
CURRENT PRICE $10.00

FOR ADDITIONAL COPIES WRITE:

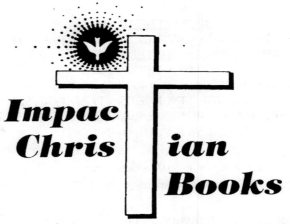

Impac **Chris** **ian** **Books**

332 Leffingwell Ave., Suite 101
Kirkwood, MO 63122

AVAILABLE AT YOUR LOCAL BOOKSTORE, OR YOU MAY ORDER DIRECTLY. Toll-Free, order-line only M/C, DISC, or VISA 1-800-451-2708.